I AM BETTER THAN YOUR KIDS

MADDOX

Art Direction & Photography:
Marie Barr

GALLERY BOOKS

New York London Toronto Sydney New Delhi

G

Gallery Books
A Division of Simon & Schuster, Inc.
1230 Avenue of the Americas
New York, NY 10020

First Gallery Books hardcover edition November 2011

GALLERY BOOKS and colophon are registered trademarks of Simon & Schuster, Inc.

For information about special discounts for bulk purchases, please contact Simon & Schuster Special Sales at 1-866-506-1949 or business@simonandschuster.com.

The Simon & Schuster Speakers Bureau can bring authors to your live event. For more information or to book an event contact the Simon & Schuster Speakers Bureau at 1-866-248-3049 or visit our website at www.simonspeakers.com.

Manufactured in the United States of America

10 9 8 7 6 5 4 3 2 1

Library of Congress Cataloging-in-Publication Data is available.

ISBN 978-1-4391-8286-4
ISBN 978-1-4391-8287-1 (ebook)

To the only person I know who's had two books dedicated to him: Me.

Contents

Introduction

"These are the drawings of little 6—8 year olds! Of course they can't draw better than you, they're kids! What's your fucking problem?"

—Anonymous hater

Several years ago, I was waiting in a coworker's cubicle when I noticed the drawings she had on display, and I told her they sucked. She gasped and said, "They were made by my four-year-old nephew!" So I elaborated, "Well, your nephew sucks at drawing." I decided then that kids had gotten a free pass for far too long. So on my website, I proceeded to grade a handful of children's art, along with some pointed, but fair, criticism.

The response was overwhelming.

By the end of the month, more than 6 million people had read it, and tens of millions more have read it since. Ever wonder where all those emails that your friends forward to you come from? I happen to know, because I am one of the unsung geniuses whose work becomes the bastard child of Gmail accounts across the web. The email forward in which I graded crappy children's artwork, titled "I am better than your kids," went viral in 2002 and was the first introduction most people had to my writing. It circulated to the point where some of my friends unknowingly forwarded it to me, asking why I couldn't write anything that brilliant. I also received thousands of emails per day from supportive grade school teachers, who said I'd given them voice, as well as from a few U.S. Department of Defense officials, who probably should have been doing something better with their time. The article had become a phenomenon.

Then came the backlash.

I got hundreds of thousands of emails, some of which criticized me for grading the children harshly. I was accused of ageism—someone who discriminates based on age. The most common criticism I received was, "How dare you criticize kids? They're children! Of course they can't draw as well as you can, asshole!"

The irony is that, I'm actually not being ageist. By using the same standard to judge a child's art as I would an adult's, I'm treating them with equality. If a kid wants to impress me, he has to draw something awesome, just like an adult would. Kids don't get a free pass just for being kids. In fact, the only way to treat kids fairly is to expect the same standards of excellence as you would anyone else.

Good Job

The two most dangerous words in the English language are: "good job." It's a quick little lie that parents tell their kids to encourage them to keep trying. Parents are afraid that if they tell their kids the truth, they'll get discouraged and stop drawing. So what? More kids need to be discouraged. Since when is every kid supposed to be able to draw? Think about your own life for a moment. Of all the people you know, how many of them are artists, professionally? How many of them do something even tangentially related to art? For most people, that number is zero. According to the Bureau of Labor Statistics, fine artists (including painters, sculptors, and illustrators) held about 23,600 jobs in 2008. With the U.S. Census Bureau estimating 307 million people in the US in 2009, only .008% are artists. You probably don't know any artists. Statistically speaking, nobody does.

Somewhere between the time parents first gush undue praise and college, the law of diminishing returns kicks in. At a certain point, no amount of encouragement will make someone any better at art. That's when something wonderful happens to these kids: they realize that they suck. Just as no amount of encouragement alone can make someone an airline pilot, mechanical engineer, or heart surgeon, kids come to realize they're not actually artists.

So why art? Why is this the one discipline that parents feel necessary to push upon their kids? Why not mechanical engineering? Why do you never see parents handing a kid some graph paper, a calculator, and a copy of Newton's *Principia*? Oh, I know! Because encouraging kids to keep trying something they suck at—or aren't interested in—is a waste of time.

The only exceptions to this rule are reading, writing, and arithmetic. These skills are necessary for communication and understanding of all higher levels of education that succeed them. Visual art is not. Painting and drawing are forms of expression, and disingenuous support gives the child a disincentive to become better. Creators who can endure critics are the only ones who deserve to be creators. That is, anyone whose resolve is too weak to weather criticism of his or her art, shouldn't be creating art. I've read tens of thousands of emails criticizing me over the years, for everything from my writing, grammar, style, penis size, clothing, hygiene, friends (or lack thereof), family and my receding hairline, to my sexual prowess and orientation (I've been accused of being a "gay faggot," performing fellatio, and being a virgin all in the same paragraph). I've heard it all. And yet, I still create, because it's what I love to do. I don't need anyone to pat me on the ass and say "good job" to keep writing. In fact, both of my parents have begged me to stop. My mom even prayed that I would get cancer before going on my last book tour. She hoped that my book would fail, I'd go bankrupt, and that my writing career would end in disaster. Ironically, nothing could have encouraged me more to succeed, because my success is the biggest "fuck you" to my mom, my high school teachers, the writing department at the University of Utah, and everyone who's ever discouraged me in life. By not criticizing kids, you're depriving them of the opportunity to become truly great, like me.

What's worse is that all this superfluous praise is making the world a duller place. The phrase "good job" is the reason we don't have any more Mozarts or Beethovens today. Mozart's father never coddled him with heaps of praise when he didn't deserve it, and that hard-earned praise was part of what motivated Mozart to constantly push harder and to make some of the most enduring music the world has ever heard. In fact, I'm not sure even *Mozart*'s father pushed hard enough. Sure his music is great, but let's face it: Mozart could have done more with his life. He died penniless, had few mourners, and was unceremoniously tossed in an unmarked grave. While musically a genius, he was a fuckup who mismanaged his money and liked shit jokes. He had no business sense, and he wasn't able to sell himself—or his music—to any appreciable degree for any significant amount of time. It was only in death that he gained notoriety, and scholars today still struggle to explain away and contextualize his fixation on scatological humor. Historians can't come to terms with the fact that Mozart was kind of a fuckup, which is why there's an entire Wikipedia page devoted to Mozart's scatological jokes and what higher meaning they may have. Sometimes a shit joke is just a shit joke.

So you're welcome. By holding kids to a higher standard, I'm making the world a better place. Although many of the names in this book have been changed to keep the children anonymous, some were kept the same, as it is my sincere hope that at least a few kids recognize their artwork and try harder next time. The last thing this world needs is more cocksure idiots who think they're producing great works of art because their parents did them the disservice of encouragement.

Special Cars from Special Kids

Jon, age 8

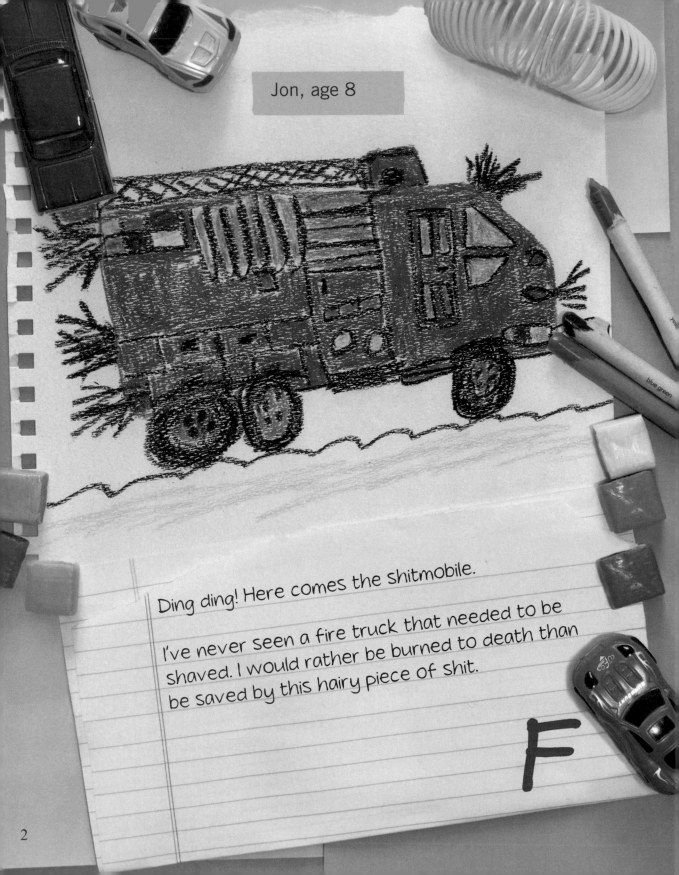

Ding ding! Here comes the Shitmobile.

I've never seen a fire truck that needed to be shaved. I would rather be burned to death than be saved by this hairy piece of shit.

F

2

prison

Arcade

Robert, age 5

Finally, a car with both an arcade and a prison! Back when cars had just arcades in them, there was no place to lock up kids who got out of line.

F+

Lane, age 4

I created a list of pros and cons for this car:

Pros:	Cons:
✓ Roomy	✗ Wagon wheels
	✗ Only one door
	✗ The hinges on the door are on the outside.
	✗ Entire rear end seems to emit exhaust.

F

3

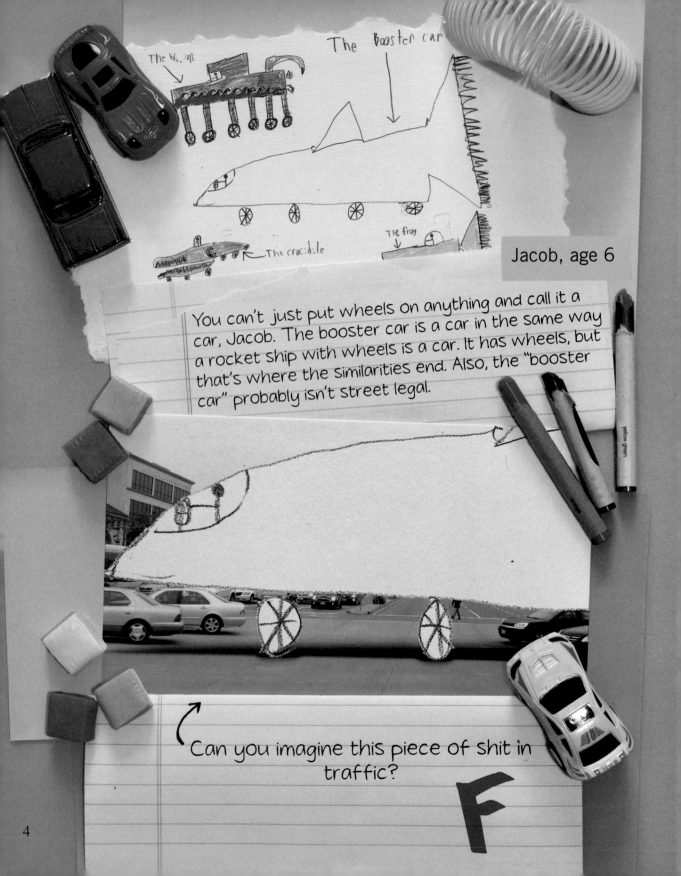

The Worm

The Booster car

The crocidile

The frog

Jacob, age 6

You can't just put wheels on anything and call it a car, Jacob. The booster car is a car in the same way a rocket ship with wheels is a car. It has wheels, but that's where the similarities end. Also, the "booster car" probably isn't street legal.

Can you imagine this piece of shit in traffic?

F

4

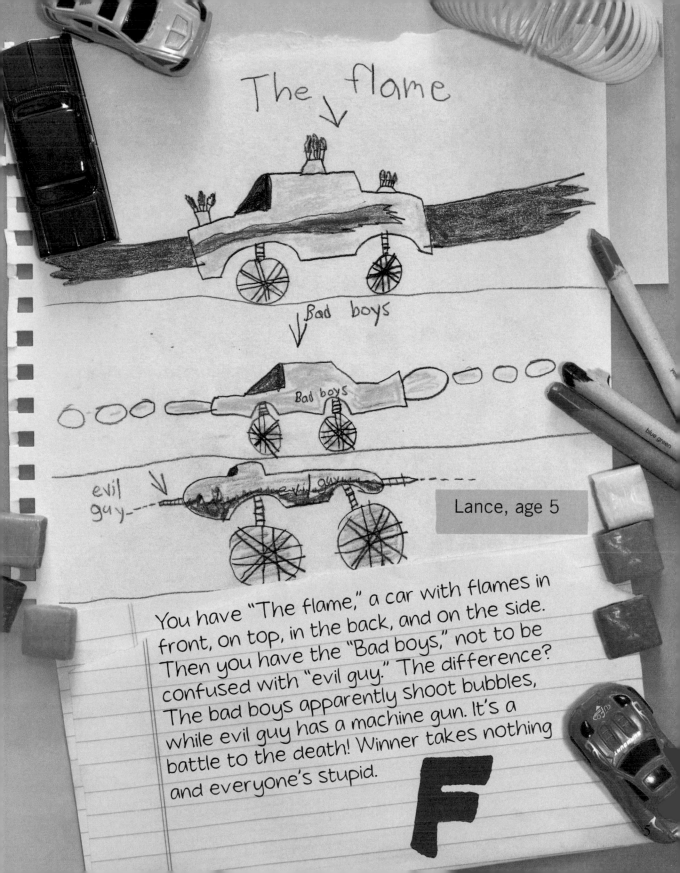

The flame

Bad boys

Bad boys

evil guy

evil guy

Lance, age 5

You have "The flame," a car with flames in front, on top, in the back, and on the side. Then you have the "Bad boys," not to be confused with "evil guy." The difference? The bad boys apparently shoot bubbles, while evil guy has a machine gun. It's a battle to the death! Winner takes nothing and everyone's stupid.

F

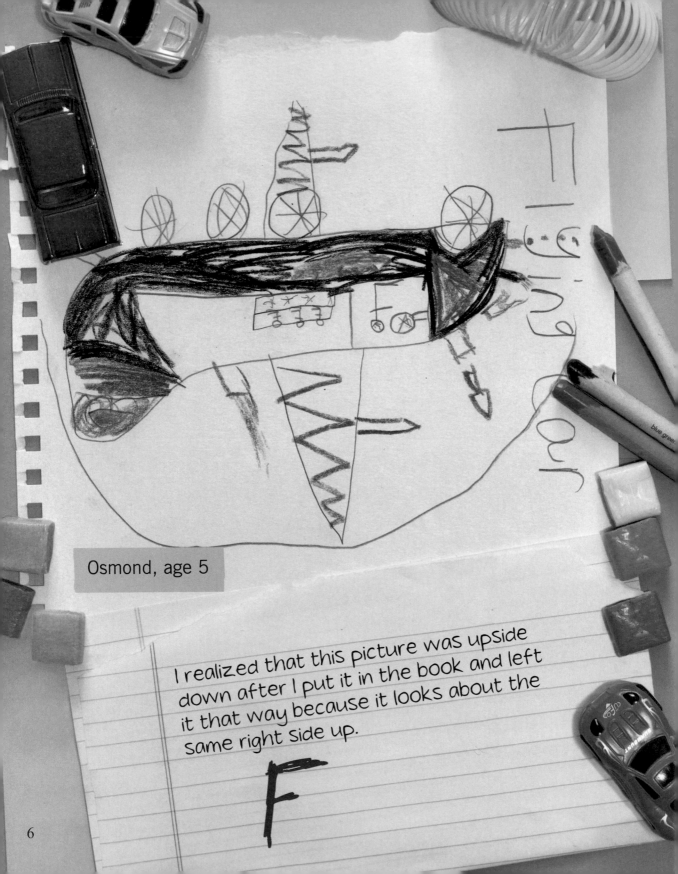

Osmond, age 5

I realized that this picture was upside down after I put it in the book and left it that way because it looks about the same right side up.

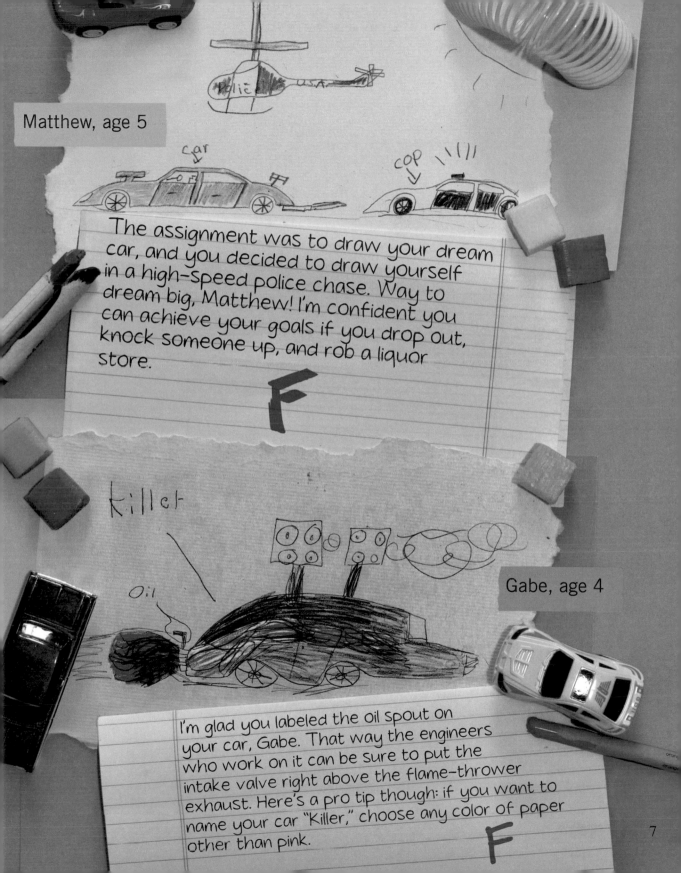

Matthew, age 5

car

cop

Police U.S.A.

The assignment was to draw your dream car, and you decided to draw yourself in a high-speed police chase. Way to dream big, Matthew! I'm confident you can achieve your goals if you drop out, knock someone up, and rob a liquor store.

F

killer

Oil

Gabe, age 4

I'm glad you labeled the oil spout on your car, Gabe. That way the engineers who work on it can be sure to put the intake valve right above the flame-thrower exhaust. Here's a pro tip though: if you want to name your car "Killer," choose any color of paper other than pink.

F

Eduardo, age 6

It was only a matter of time before some misguided kid drew the Ed Hardy "Love Kills Slowly" slogan on a war machine. This critique isn't for the artwork so much as the logo—which was drawn perfectly. It's easily the worst part of this drawing, which is saying something considering the kid drew himself as a ski-masked, machine-gun-toting terrorist.

F

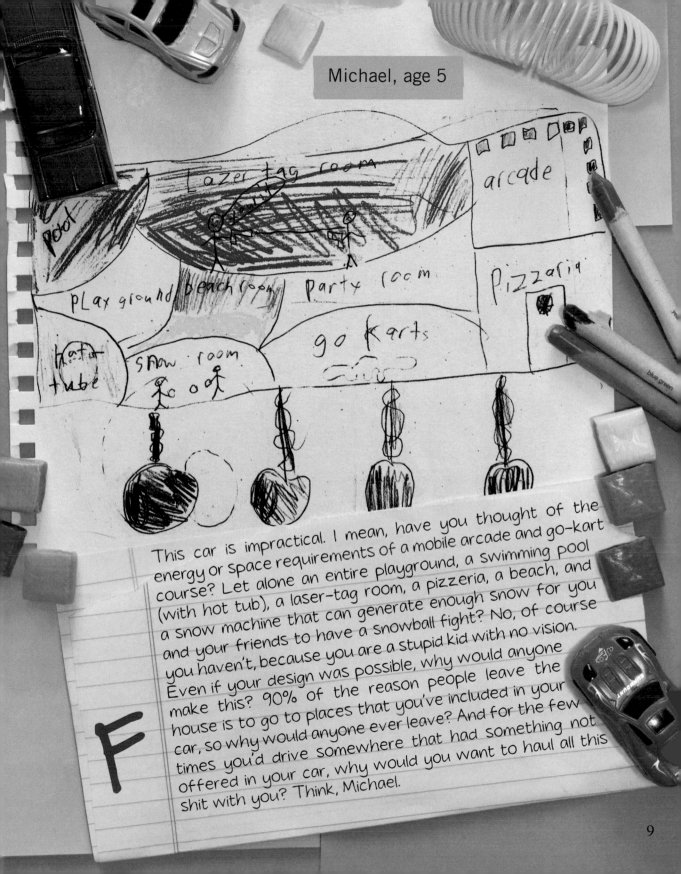

Michael, age 5

This car is impractical. I mean, have you thought of the energy or space requirements of a mobile arcade and go-kart course? Let alone an entire playground, a swimming pool (with hot tub), a laser-tag room, a pizzeria, a beach, and a snow machine that can generate enough snow for you and your friends to have a snowball fight? No, of course you haven't, because you are a stupid kid with no vision. Even if your design was possible, why would anyone make this? 90% of the reason people leave the house is to go to places that you've included in your car, so why would anyone ever leave? And for the few times you'd drive somewhere that had something not offered in your car, why would you want to haul all this shit with you? Think, Michael.

F

Sliver Bullet

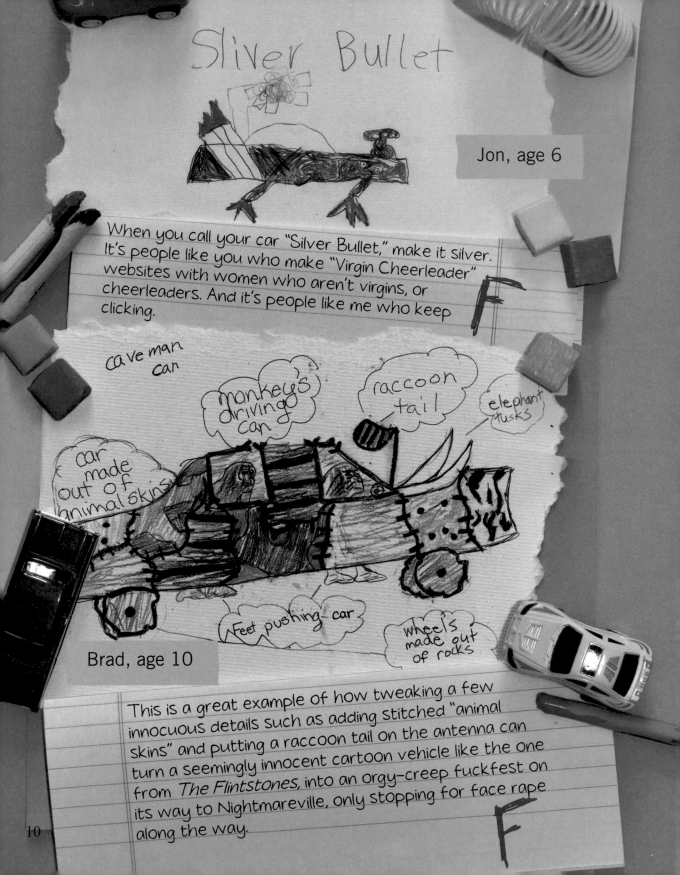

Jon, age 6

When you call your car "Silver Bullet," make it silver. It's people like you who make "Virgin Cheerleader" websites with women who aren't virgins, or cheerleaders. And it's people like me who keep clicking.

caveman car

monkeys driving car

raccoon tail

elephant tusks

car made out of animal skins

Feet pushing car

wheels made out of rocks

Brad, age 10

This is a great example of how tweaking a few innocuous details such as adding stitched "animal skins" and putting a raccoon tail on the antenna can turn a seemingly innocent cartoon vehicle like the one from *The Flintstones*, into an orgy-creep fuckfest on its way to Nightmareville, only stopping for face rape along the way.

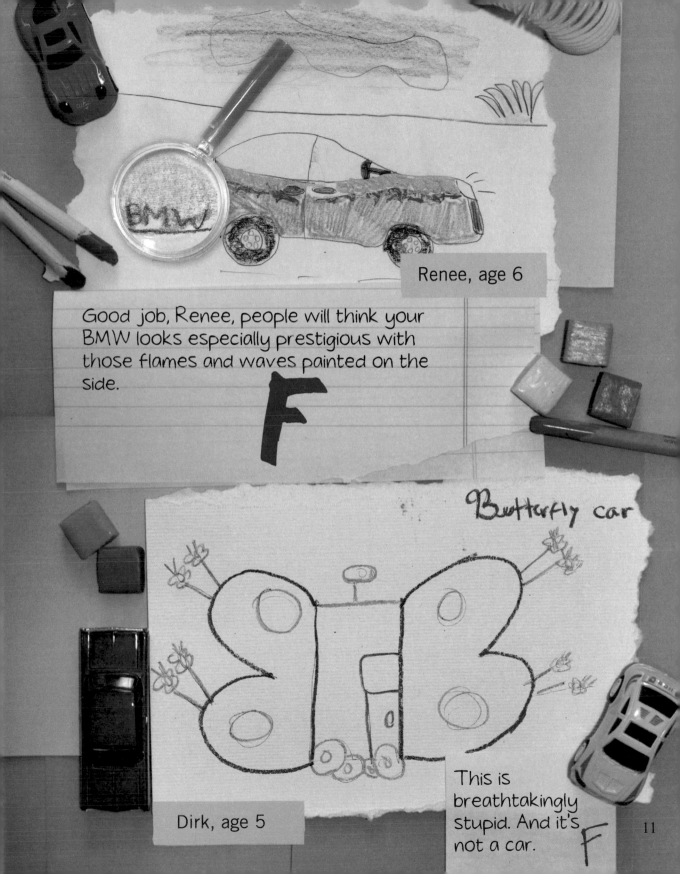

Renee, age 6

Good job, Renee, people will think your BMW looks especially prestigious with those flames and waves painted on the side.

F

Butterfly car

Dirk, age 5

This is breathtakingly stupid. And it's not a car.

F

11

Convertble Car!

Nathan, age 5

There are only two requirements to drawing a convertible car:

1. that it's a car
2. that it's a convertible

You failed to meet 50% of the requirements.

F

Navy Camerio 7,000

JC, age 8

"General, the enemy sent their war machine. WAIT! Is that a giant saw blade fixed to a long fishing pole in front? HOLY FUCK! This can mean only one thing: this is the navy Camerio 7,000!!!!!"—something nobody will ever say.

F

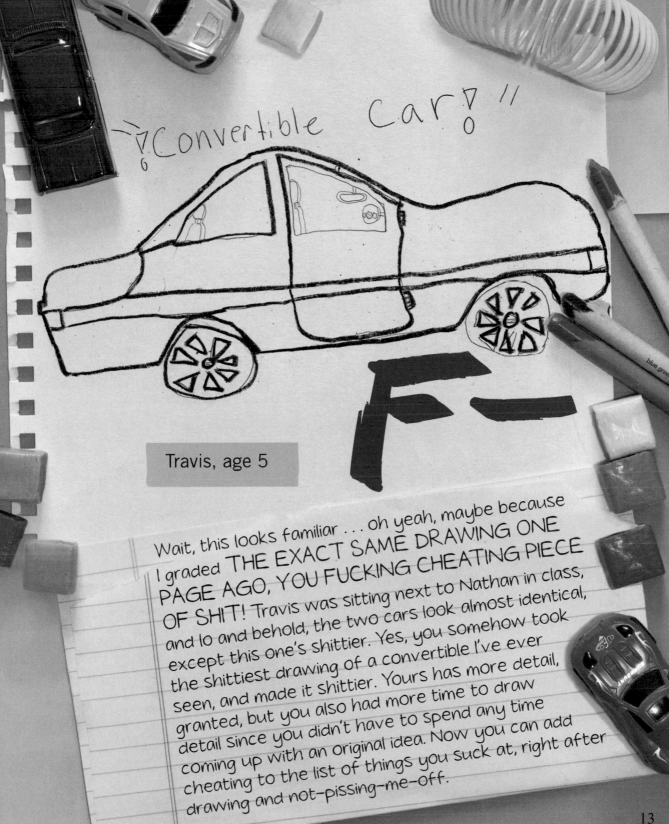

"Convertible Car"

Travis, age 5

F−

Wait, this looks familiar . . . oh yeah, maybe because I graded THE EXACT SAME DRAWING ONE PAGE AGO, YOU FUCKING CHEATING PIECE OF SHIT! Travis was sitting next to Nathan in class, and lo and behold, the two cars look almost identical, except this one's shittier. Yes, you somehow took the shittiest drawing of a convertible I've ever seen, and made it shittier. Yours has more detail, granted, but you also had more time to draw since you didn't have to spend any time coming up with an original idea. Now you can add cheating to the list of things you suck at, right after drawing and not-pissing-me-off.

13

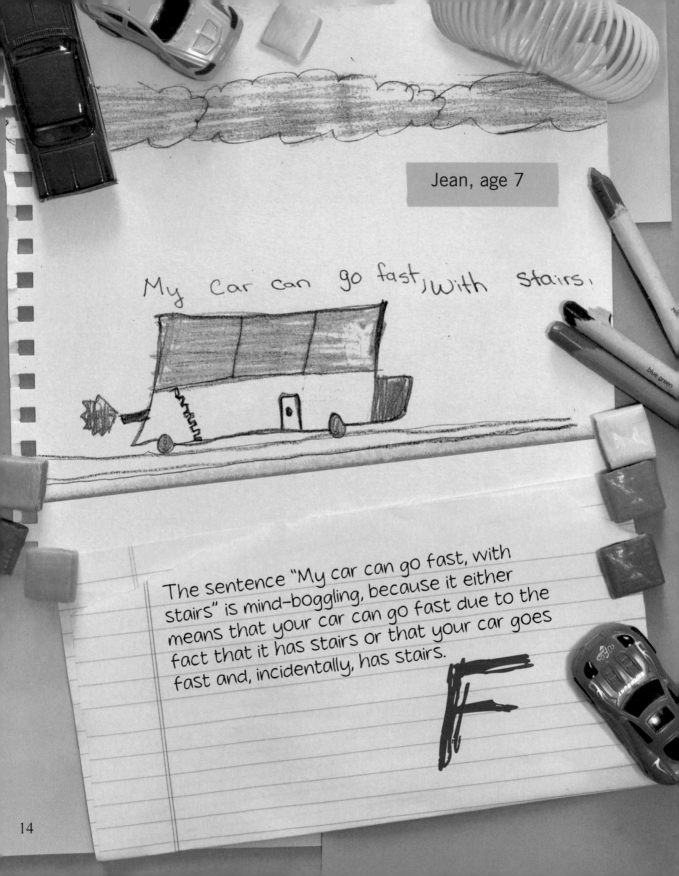

My car can go fast, with stairs.

Jean, age 7

The sentence "My car can go fast, with stairs" is mind-boggling, because it either means that your car can go fast due to the fact that it has stairs or that your car goes fast and, incidentally, has stairs.

F

14

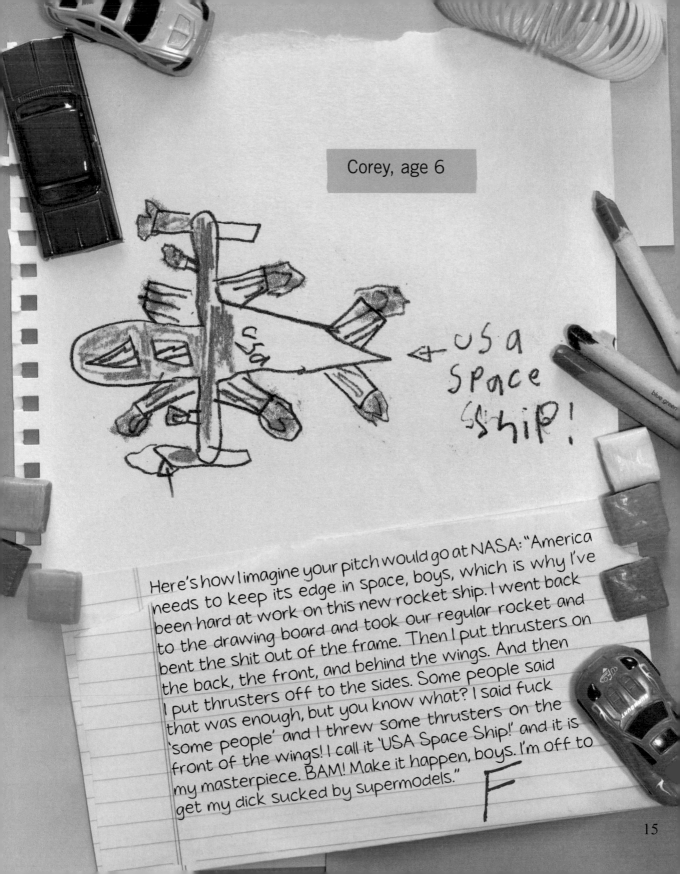

Corey, age 6

←USA Space Sship!

Here's how I imagine your pitch would go at NASA: "America needs to keep its edge in space, boys, which is why I've been hard at work on this new rocket ship. I went back to the drawing board and took our regular rocket and bent the shit out of the frame. Then I put thrusters on the back, the front, and behind the wings. And then I put thrusters off to the sides. Some people said that was enough, but you know what? I said fuck 'some people' and I threw some thrusters on the front of the wings! I call it 'USA Space Ship!' and it is my masterpiece. BAM! Make it happen, boys. I'm off to get my dick sucked by supermodels."

F

15

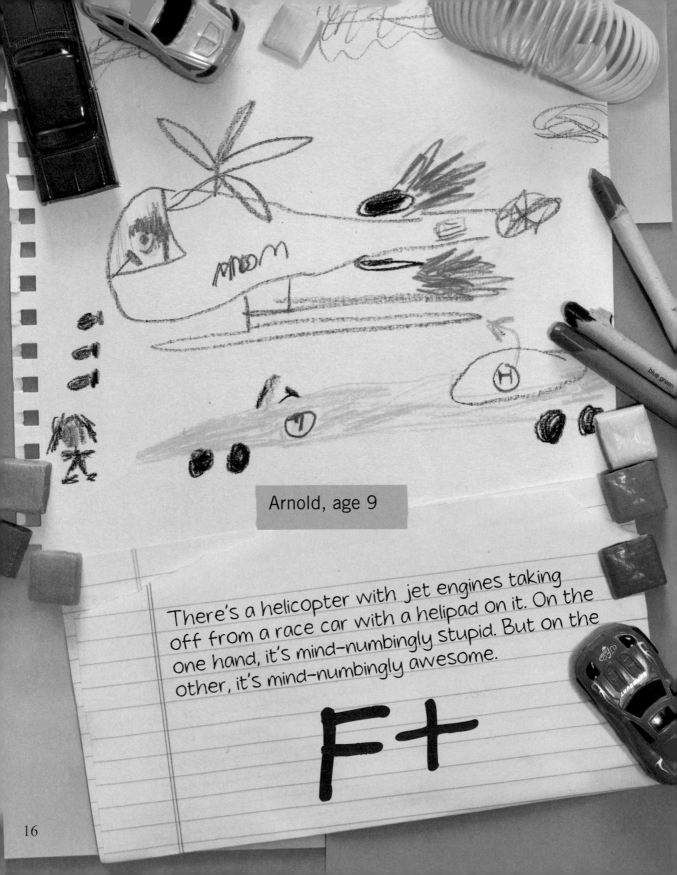

Arnold, age 9

There's a helicopter with jet engines taking off from a race car with a helipad on it. On the one hand, it's mind-numbingly stupid. But on the other, it's mind-numbingly awesome.

F+

16

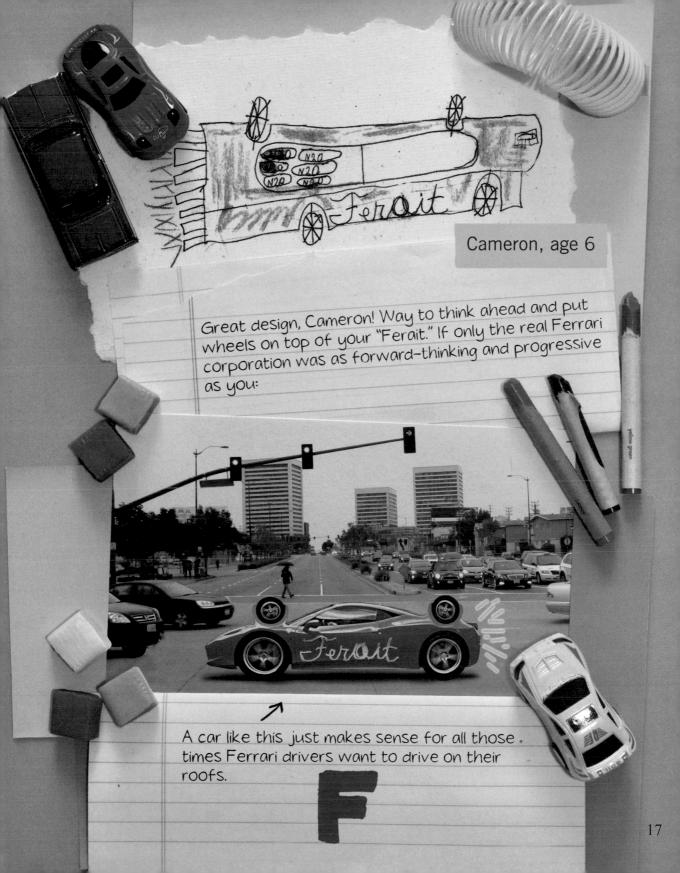

Cameron, age 6

Great design, Cameron! Way to think ahead and put wheels on top of your "Ferait." If only the real Ferrari corporation was as forward-thinking and progressive as you:

A car like this just makes sense for all those times Ferrari drivers want to drive on their roofs.

Grave Digger

When I think of the monster truck Grave Digger, I think of the black and purple cabin with green suspension, giant tires, and a badass skull on the side. Not a sunshine-yellow Scion xB with a hood ornament that looks like a heart. Barf.

F

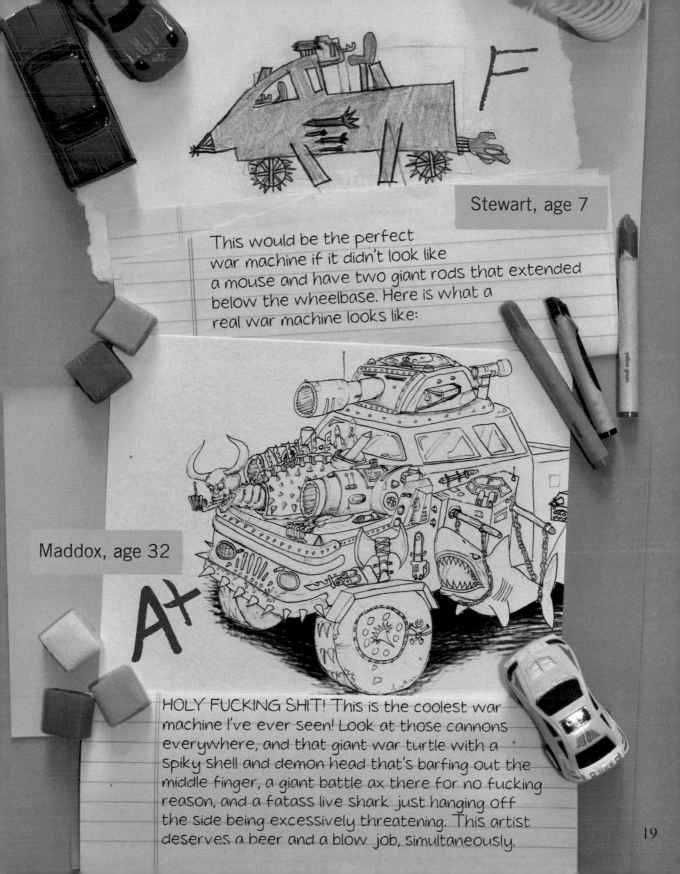

Stewart, age 7

This would be the perfect war machine if it didn't look like a mouse and have two giant rods that extended below the wheelbase. Here is what a real war machine looks like:

Maddox, age 32

A+

HOLY FUCKING SHIT! This is the coolest war machine I've ever seen! Look at those cannons everywhere, and that giant war turtle with a spiky shell and demon head that's barfing out the middle finger, a giant battle ax there for no fucking reason, and a fatass live shark just hanging off the side being excessively threatening. This artist deserves a beer and a blow job, simultaneously.

19

Unintentional Hitler

Nadi, age 7

Oops! Although you meant to draw a suburban housewife, what you actually drew was the most brutal dictator in history. That is a very unfortunately placed eraser smudge, but the Hitleresque comb-over put it over the top.

F

21

Führer the Hedghog.

Wayne, age 7

Nadi, age 7

"Oh nothing, just hanging out in front of my house, looking at butterflies flying in front of my swastika window. 'Sup with you?"

22

Greg, age 7

Hitler on a tractor is one of those surreal thoughts that pop into your head when you're bored while waiting for your dentist appointment, and you start daydreaming about all the mundane things Hitler had to do on a daily basis, like frying eggs, flossing, and folding his pants.

23

Sean, age 7

Some people play catch in the park. Others salute Nazis. Everyone is different.

F

MEIN AUGE !!

Josef, age 6

Hitler Mr. Potato Head getting pissed in the eye. Awesome.

F+

Remie, age 9

"I got a toy train set, what did you get?" "I got a twenty-five-point plan for expelling Jews from eastern Europe."

F

25

Eric, age 8

Lovely day at the park with Papa Adolf and his family, frolicking under a rainbow.

F

26

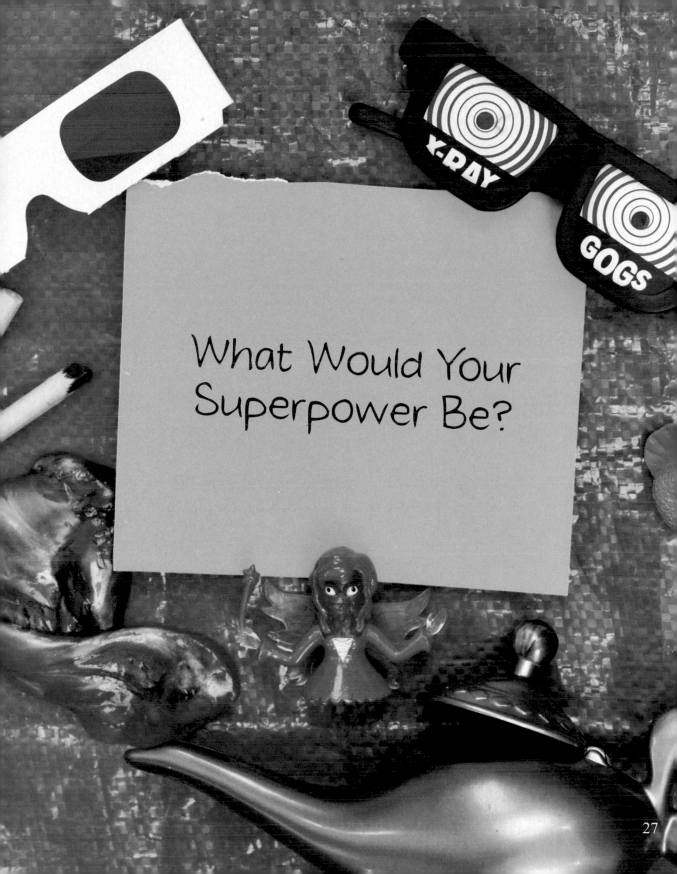

What Would Your
Superpower Be?

27

All powers

F

K

Super D

When I was a kid, I used to draw myself as a superhero with special powers* and compare it to my friends' drawings. It's fun until some shithead inevitably chooses "all powers" for his special ability and ruins the game, Damon.

When Peter Parker created his alter ego to strike fear into the hearts of criminals, I doubt "spread eagled with a constipated expression" is what he had in mind.

F

Cole, age 7

*Still do.

Sara, age 7

I am imbisible

F

I once had a smudge on my monitor and I left it there for so long that I started to rearrange the icons on my desktop around it instead of cleaning it. That's pretty lazy, but this "imbisible" drawing is laziness of a higher order. Even the Invisible Woman from Fantastic 4 has dotted lines drawn around her to establish things like scale, where she is in relation to other things, or whether or not she even exists. But no, not Sara. And even if you wanted to "draw" an invisible woman with nothing, why isn't there anything else in the scene? It's an invisible woman, not an invisible universe.

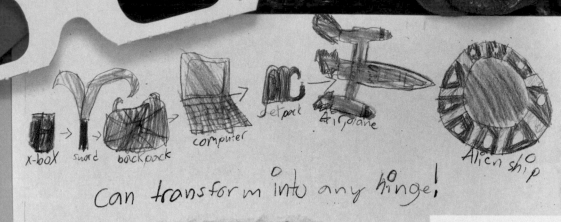

x-box → sword → backpack

computer

jetpack

Airplane

Alien ship

Can transform into any hinge!

Stewart, age 7

The power to transform into "any hinge" is a power beyond imagination, in the sense that it's a power nobody wants to imagine. Also, none of the things you drew here is actually a hinge.

F

I could fly!!!

When you imagine a world in which you have the miracle of flight at your whim, what do you do? You drop a cat hurtling down toward earth. I can actually get behind this.

F+

Genevive, age 7

LASER BEAM
SPEEPEY
SPEEPEY
DOUG

Laser Beam

SPY
Jounirs
SQUAD

DOUG
SPY

Tune in for the exciting adventures of the "SPY Jounirs SQUAD." Featuring Laser Beam with the power of a concentrated laser blast; Speedey, able to go faster than lightning; and Doug. Doug has no special abilities and isn't even as tall as the other Jounir Squad members. Toy companies everywhere can't wait to pass on this shitty franchise.

F

Monika, age 8

you cant see me

F

Yes, I can. Also, the assignment was to name your superpower, not to state its effect. If all superheroes used your naming convention, Spider-Man would be called "the Amazing I-Will-Capture-You-in-My-Web."

the AMAZING I-WILL-CAPTURE YOU-IN-MY-WEB

$1.25 US
$900 CAN

MAD DOX

If superpowe warh would it will be
and yie

IF i had a super powe it woll
be .3Metel bons will come out
Of my fist and my in tier bones
will be metel. I would be
indestruktibull and when I get cut
the cut will helle super fast.

I will cut logs, sadwiches, and
I could stik them out when
ever I want to. And i could cut
threw walls. And i would discis
me self as a wolfman. And
have a chopermotersicel. And
you could smell thig a 100 yards
away and instras.

Jason, age 9

". . . and I would call this superhero: Wolferine!
It's totally different from Wolverine. You
see, Wolverine has a skeleton covered in the
indestructible alloy adamantium. My skeleton
would be covered in 'metel,' that is 'indestruktibull.'
And whereas Wolverine fights villains with his
metal claws, I will cut logs and sandwiches
with my metel bars."

33

Developmentally Challenged
Developments

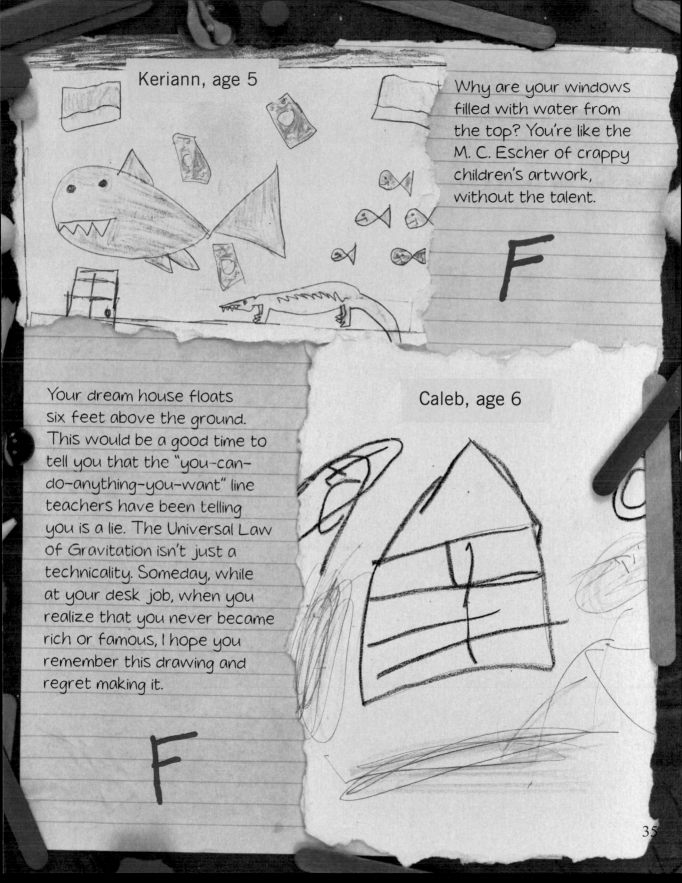

Keriann, age 5

Why are your windows filled with water from the top? You're like the M. C. Escher of crappy children's artwork, without the talent.

F

Your dream house floats six feet above the ground. This would be a good time to tell you that the "you-can-do-anything-you-want" line teachers have been telling you is a lie. The Universal Law of Gravitation isn't just a technicality. Someday, while at your desk job, when you realize that you never became rich or famous, I hope you remember this drawing and regret making it.

F

Caleb, age 6

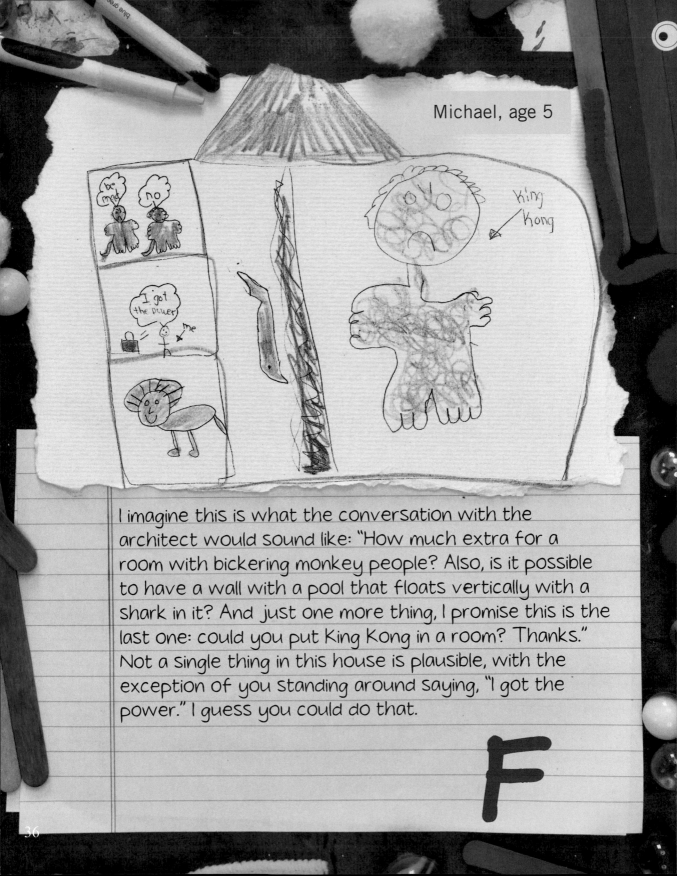

Michael, age 5

I imagine this is what the conversation with the architect would sound like: "How much extra for a room with bickering monkey people? Also, is it possible to have a wall with a pool that floats vertically with a shark in it? And just one more thing, I promise this is the last one: could you put King Kong in a room? Thanks." Not a single thing in this house is plausible, with the exception of you standing around saying, "I got the power." I guess you could do that.

F

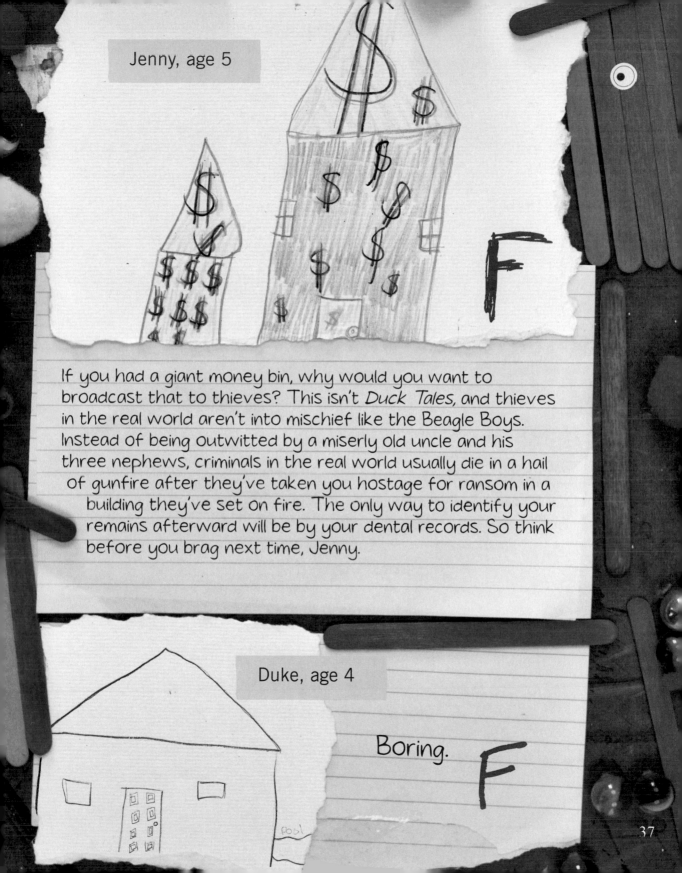

Jenny, age 5

F

If you had a giant money bin, why would you want to broadcast that to thieves? This isn't *Duck Tales,* and thieves in the real world aren't into mischief like the Beagle Boys. Instead of being outwitted by a miserly old uncle and his three nephews, criminals in the real world usually die in a hail of gunfire after they've taken you hostage for ransom in a building they've set on fire. The only way to identify your remains afterward will be by your dental records. So think before you brag next time, Jenny.

Duke, age 4

Boring. F

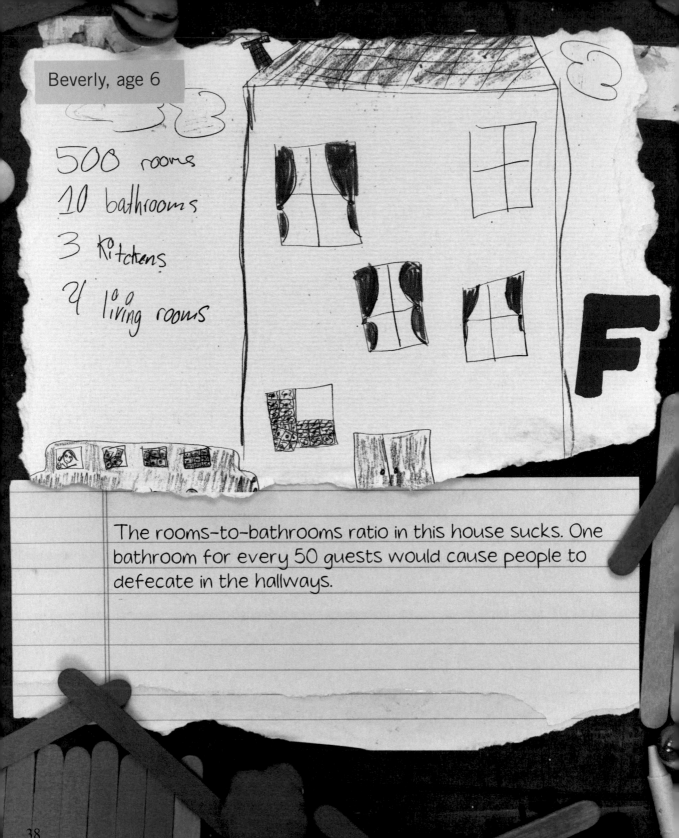

Beverly, age 6

500 rooms
10 bathrooms
3 kitchens
4 living rooms

The rooms-to-bathrooms ratio in this house sucks. One bathroom for every 50 guests would cause people to defecate in the hallways.

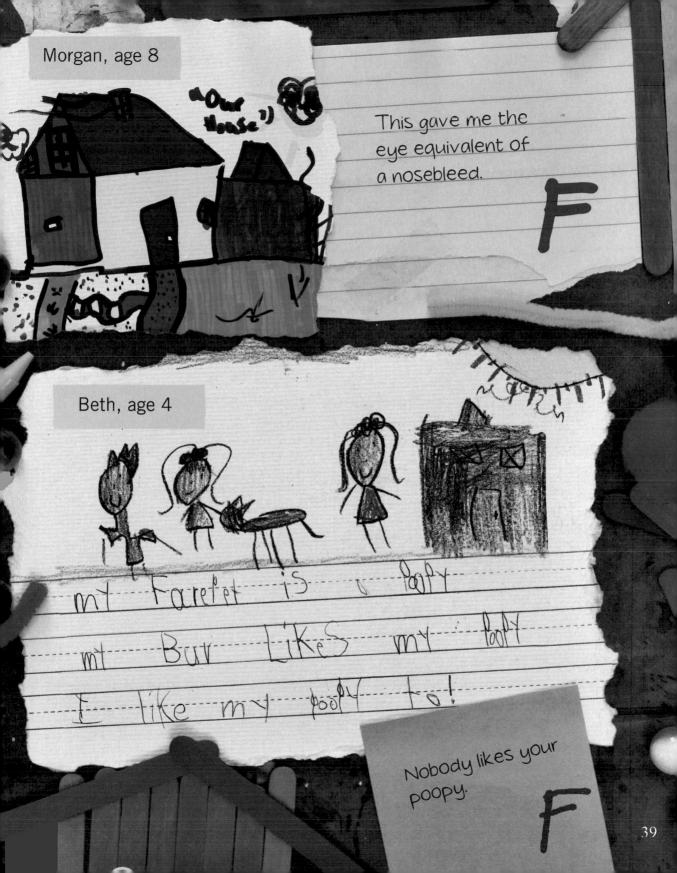

Morgan, age 8

"Our House"

This gave me the eye equivalent of a nosebleed.

F

Beth, age 4

my Farefet is a Poofy
mt Bur Likes my Poofy
I like my poofy to!

Nobody likes your poopy.

F

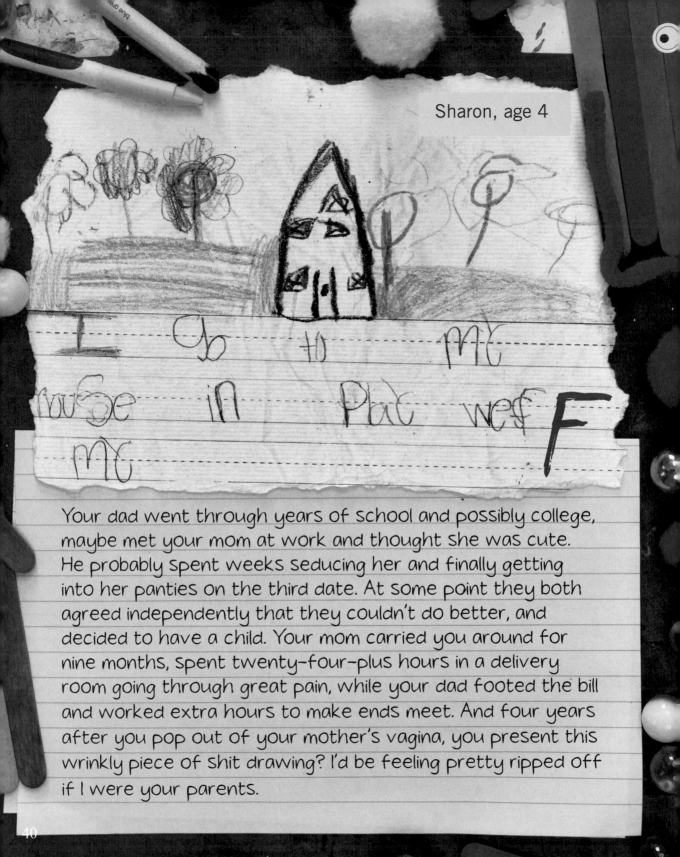

Sharon, age 4

I go to me
rouse in Plat wesf F
me

Your dad went through years of school and possibly college, maybe met your mom at work and thought she was cute. He probably spent weeks seducing her and finally getting into her panties on the third date. At some point they both agreed independently that they couldn't do better, and decided to have a child. Your mom carried you around for nine months, spent twenty-four-plus hours in a delivery room going through great pain, while your dad footed the bill and worked extra hours to make ends meet. And four years after you pop out of your mother's vagina, you present this wrinkly piece of shit drawing? I'd be feeling pretty ripped off if I were your parents.

My Map

Jeremie, age 5

f me

Google maps has nothing on this.

F

This actually seems like an appropriate house for someone of your ability. I see this house and think: the universe is just.

F+

Marshall, age 5

41

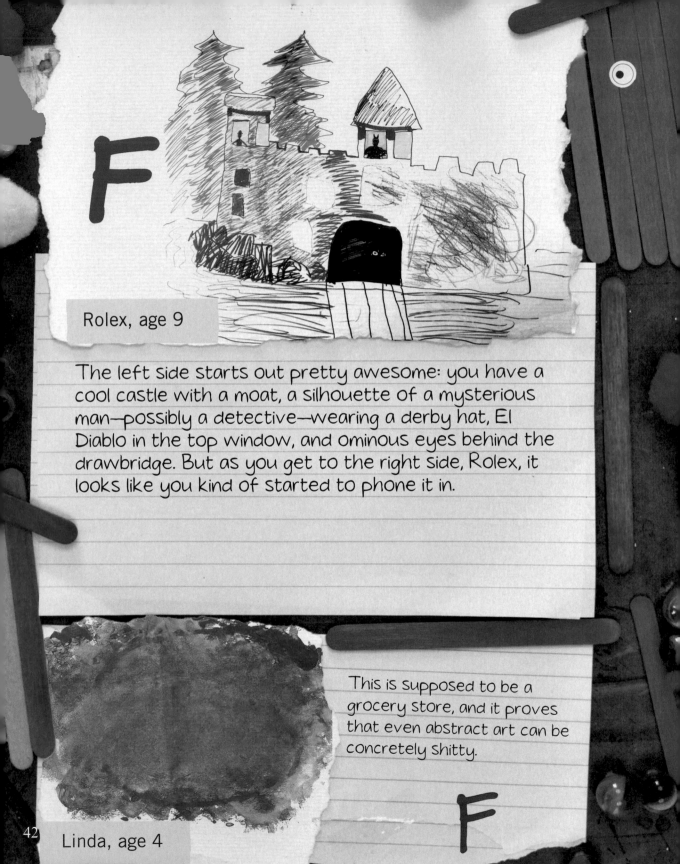

F

Rolex, age 9

The left side starts out pretty awesome: you have a cool castle with a moat, a silhouette of a mysterious man—possibly a detective—wearing a derby hat, El Diablo in the top window, and ominous eyes behind the drawbridge. But as you get to the right side, Rolex, it looks like you kind of started to phone it in.

This is supposed to be a grocery store, and it proves that even abstract art can be concretely shitty.

F

42

Linda, age 4

Jasmine, age 7

F

This was Jasmine's attempt at designing the new World Trade Center in New York. Here's how it would look in the New York skyline:

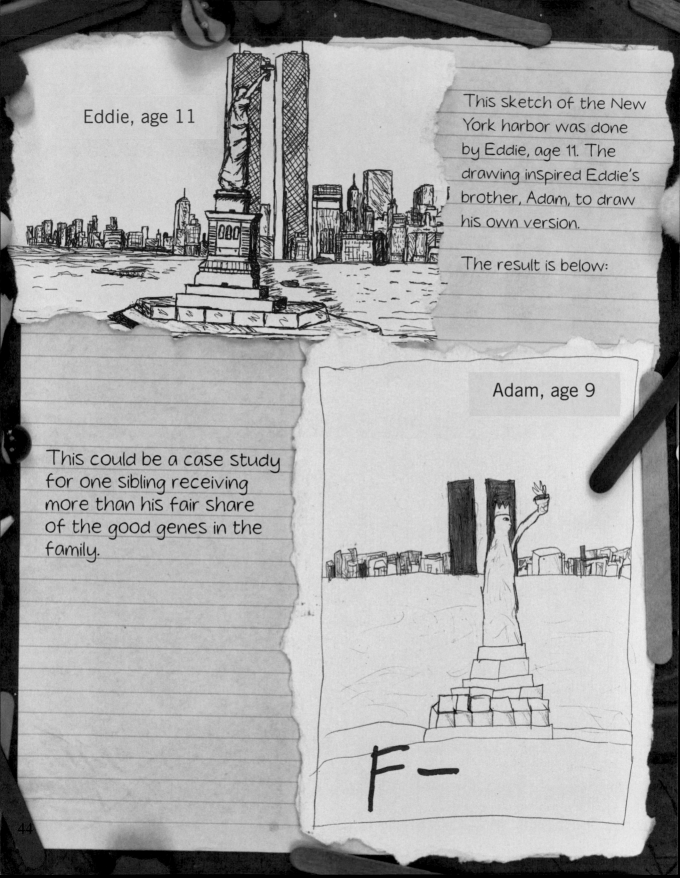

Eddie, age 11

This sketch of the New York harbor was done by Eddie, age 11. The drawing inspired Eddie's brother, Adam, to draw his own version.

The result is below:

Adam, age 9

This could be a case study for one sibling receiving more than his fair share of the good genes in the family.

F—

44

Bowls to
Throw Up In

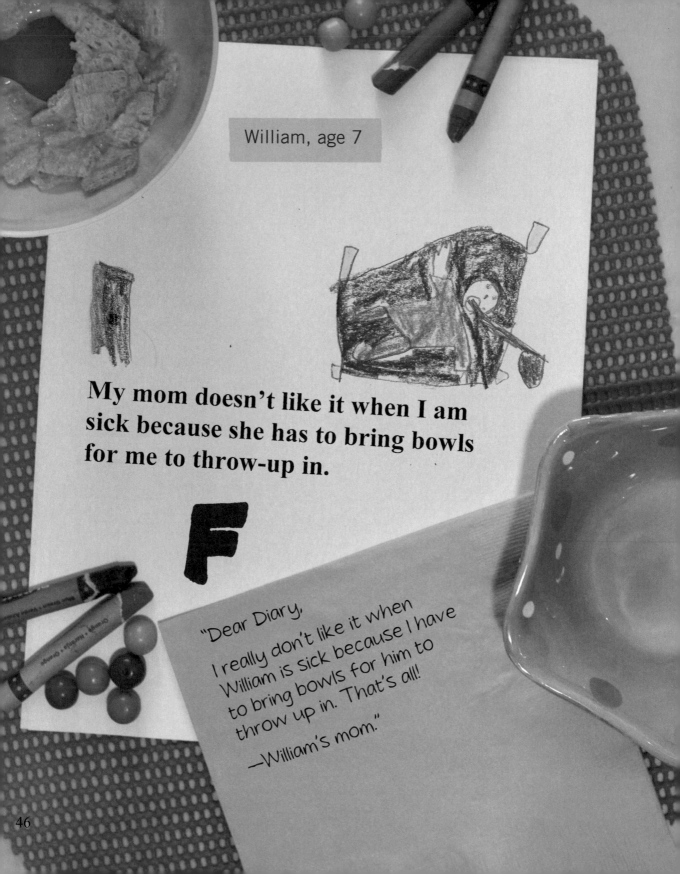

William, age 7

My mom doesn't like it when I am sick because she has to bring bowls for me to throw-up in.

F

"Dear Diary,

I really don't like it when William is sick because I have to bring bowls for him to throw up in. That's all!

—William's mom."

46

Catrina, age 10

"I brought you some soup! It's the least I could do since I make you rest in a vertical bed while you wait for your exorcism."

Dennis, age 13

Is everything okay at home, Dennis?

47

I'm for barfing on students. The rest is too crazy, in a good way. Good job.

Alien Drawings

earth

Wayland, age 7

eye moon

F

It's an alien, so let's give him one eye and a spacey name like "eye moon." Tool. But wait, how do we know it's an alien? Where's the flying saucer cliché? Deborah delivers:

Deborah, age 7

. . . and if an alien doesn't have one eye, it has to have three. There's an unspoken rule that when drawing aliens, the number of eyes must be an odd number. Yet for some reason, aliens never seem to have one arm or three. Keep being a little conformist, Deborah, and you will be able to parlay your sorority connections into a job in HR.

F

S.S. mars

Chopstick antennae? Check! Second head with impossibly fragile neck that ignores the center of gravity? You bet your ass! What exciting things won't the SS *Mars* discover with its bright pink exhaust manifold and rakishly angled nose cone?

Lilan, age 7

Alex, age 7

Earth

Neptune

I miss my hair

And in the rare case that the odd-numbered-eye rule is violated, of course the alien has to have an odd number of fingers. But that doesn't explain why Neptune is visible from Earth, or why this alien was left behind on the moon. I can only infer that Earth is "home" and Neptune is "Daddy's new apartment."

Diana, age 7

How are you this ghetto at age 7?

F

Your alien world is such a sausage fest, it could double for a strip club half a mile from the airport.

F

Lindsay, age 8

I'm not saying it's impossible for extraterrestrials to exist that represent every gay stereotype; it's just unlikely.

F

Ben, age 7

Eat pancakes

Piggy Wiggy Stiky Boy

"Greetings, Earthlings. I am Piggy Wiggy Stiky Boy. I am an alien. Our race is an arbitrarily silly one. We have an arbitrary number of extra appendages and nostrils. We can learn a lot from each other. Our race can learn about your food, culture, and music, and your race can learn about why we have Italian mustaches and love pancakes. To our mutual prosperity! Sincerely, Piggy Wiggy Stiky Boy."
—First extraterrestrial address to human race

53

Oliver, age 7

Munch, age 30

Who knew that space aliens stranded near Pluto would look like Munch's *The Scream*? Also, way to have your style competantly duplicated by a first-grader, Munch. More like butt-Munch. **F** Both of you.

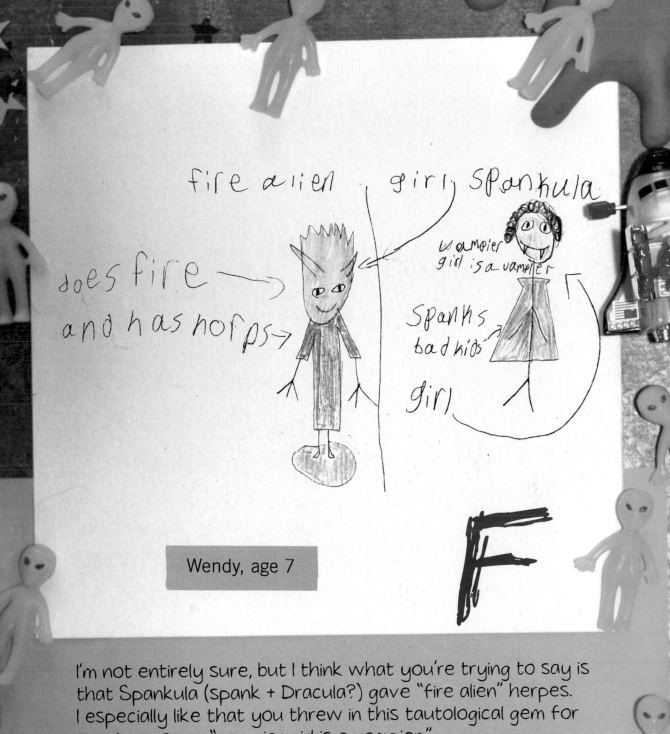

fire alien girl, Spankula

does fire →
and has horps →

wampier
girl is a vampier

spanks
bad kids →

girl

Wendy, age 7

I'm not entirely sure, but I think what you're trying to say is that Spankula (spank + Dracula?) gave "fire alien" herpes. I especially like that you threw in this tautological gem for good measure: "vampier girl is a vampier."

Melissa, age 6

him
Jesus

F

Let's start with the things you got right in this
drawing: you mostly colored inside the lines. Now
on to the wrong: there is no historical text—biblical
or otherwise—mentioning Jesus' antennae, green
arms, or lollipop.

moon

I come in peace!

chaw

Apul, age 7

I'm pretty sure the incongruity between the message "I come in peace" and the alien's facial expression wasn't intentional. You need to learn about facial expressions, Apul. Watch and learn:

F

Which of these moms would you trust to eat cookies from?[1]

Maddox, age 32

Answer: Trick question. These women have no children. And they are men.

Angela, age 3

DJ
is his
Name

F

. . . and Down's is his syndrome.

Hiroshi, age 7

100% of scientists would agree that if we should ever encounter an alien life-form, the likelihood of it resembling a Japanese rockabilly scenester is 0%.

Donna, age 8

Lame.

Hal, age 7

There doesn't seem to be a middle ground when it comes to aliens. They're either arbitrarily silly or fairly ordinary Jewish guys with no hands. Here's my take on an alien:

DON'T LOOK BELOW THIS SENTENCE UNLESS YOU WANT YOUR EYES FUCKED UP WITH A CHAIN SAW, BECAUSE THIS IS INDUSTRIAL-STRENGTH TITS.

A+

Maddox, age 32

60

Animals or ROBOTS?

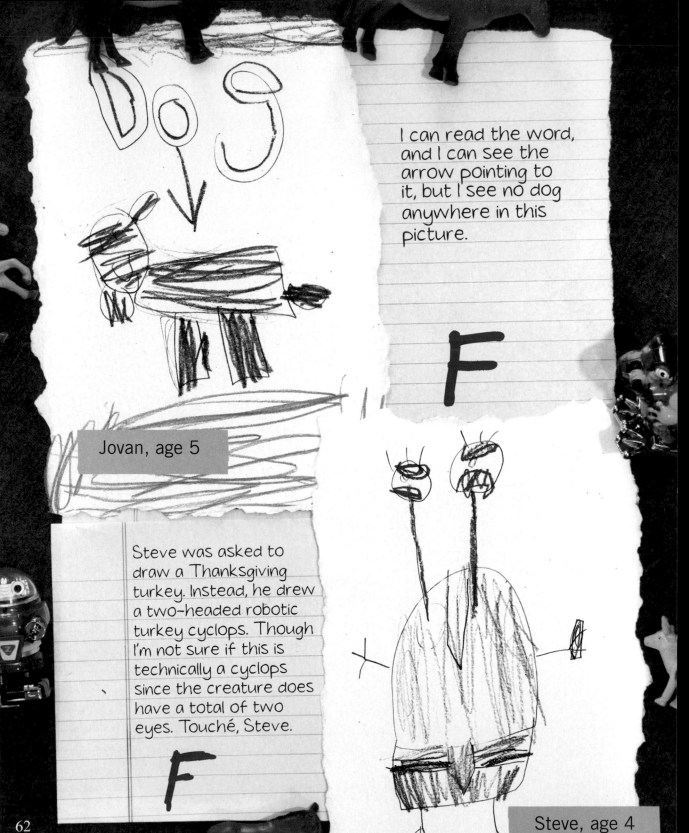

DOG

I can read the word, and I can see the arrow pointing to it, but I see no dog anywhere in this picture.

Jovan, age 5

F

Steve was asked to draw a Thanksgiving turkey. Instead, he drew a two-headed robotic turkey cyclops. Though I'm not sure if this is technically a cyclops since the creature does have a total of two eyes. Touché, Steve.

F

Steve, age 4

Ro botec horse

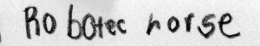

Tanner, age 8

Apparently the only difference between a "robotec" horse and a normal horse is that a robotic horse has this tiny panel below its mane:

F

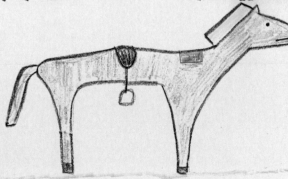

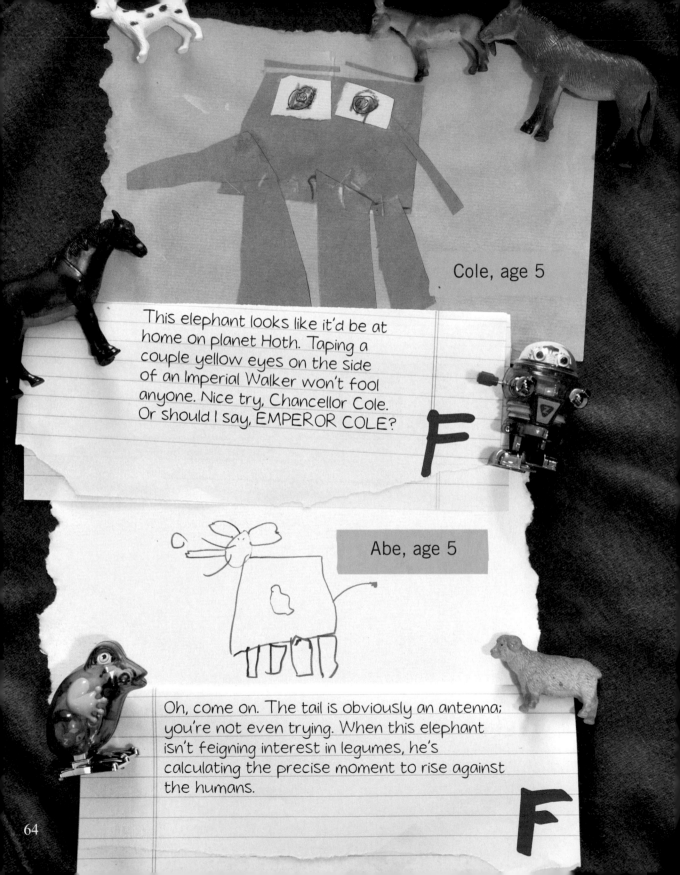

Cole, age 5

This elephant looks like it'd be at home on planet Hoth. Taping a couple yellow eyes on the side of an Imperial Walker won't fool anyone. Nice try, Chancellor Cole. Or should I say, EMPEROR COLE?

F

Abe, age 5

Oh, come on. The tail is obviously an antenna; you're not even trying. When this elephant isn't feigning interest in legumes, he's calculating the precise moment to rise against the humans.

F

Animals Fucking

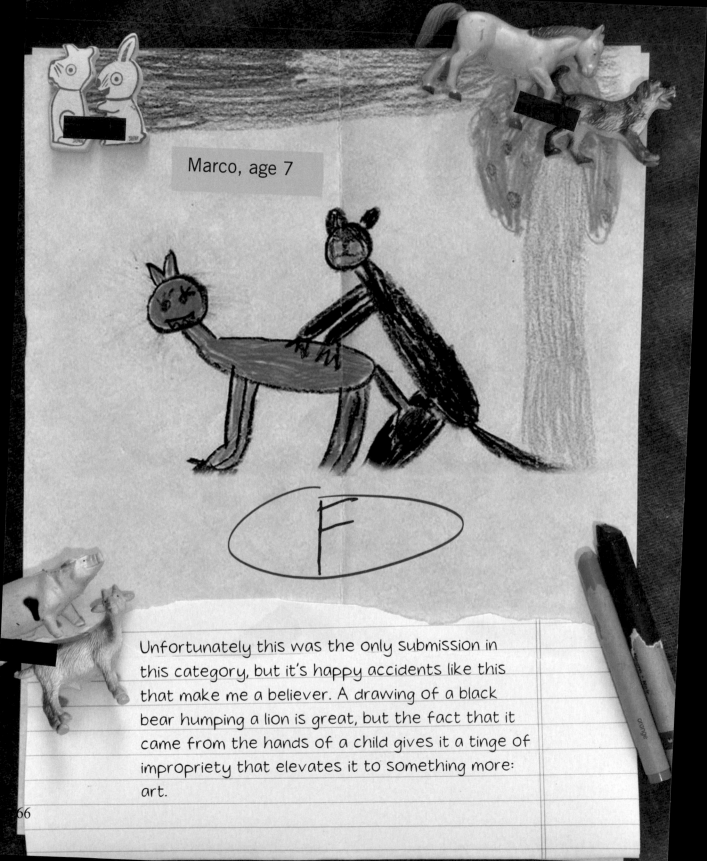

Marco, age 7

Unfortunately this was the only submission in this category, but it's happy accidents like this that make me a believer. A drawing of a black bear humping a lion is great, but the fact that it came from the hands of a child gives it a tinge of impropriety that elevates it to something more: art.

Your Favorite Holiday

my momy said
That the estr
bunny isn't rele

Jake, age 7

Yes! Your mom is awesome and I would marry her if marriage wasn't a false institution created in the Middle Ages to ensure treaties between monarchs.

F+

Fred, age 10

"Thank you for coming in for your fourth interview, Fred. This was a tough decision, but the board members here at IBM decided to hire you over the other applicants; the thing that set you apart was this drawing you made in fourth grade. When others simply drew a turkey, or a state, or a pilgrim, you drew all three. Welcome aboard, Fred! We hope you'll bring the same initiative and vision to business computing that you did with your turkey drawing!"

F

@ne wher

> If I could go en, where dering brake. The place will be China. The resen why wolud I go to china is chines food. And other resen is actiOn move's. Plues ther rock bans ther.
>
> China is, nice fun and cool bright.

Everybody knows the hottest spring break destination in the world: China! When you travel to the country, the customs officer asks you a series of questions. Here's how that conversation would go:

Customs: "Reason for visiting China?"
Maria: "Chinese food, action movies, plus rock bans. China is nice, fun, cool and bright."
Customs: "Go right ahead, ma'am. Enjoy your stay."

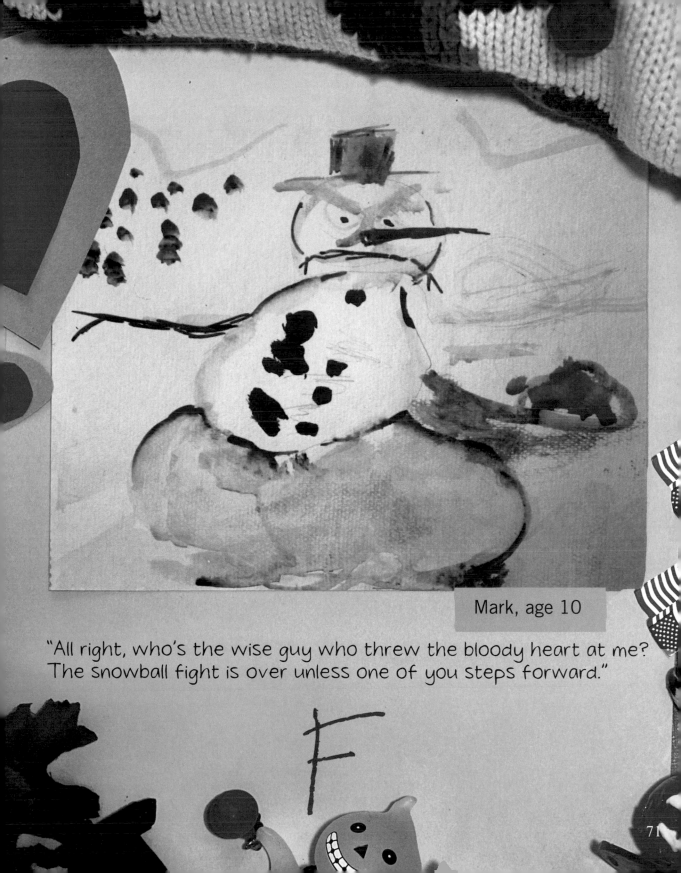

Mark, age 10

"All right, who's the wise guy who threw the bloody heart at me? The snowball fight is over unless one of you steps forward."

VALENTINES DAY

ALAN

YVMMY

Alan, age 7

What girl wouldn't love this drawing of you, Alan?
Those sharp teeth are romantic! And those dead eyes
simultaneously say, "I love you" and "braaaains."

F

Happy Brithday

F

Joanne, age 5

Birthdays aren't holidays. No one's birthday is, unless
you're a president, and even then, you had to free a ton
of slaves. And even then, your birthday gets combined with
Washington's birthday—and he planted apple trees all across
America with his giant blue ox. What did you do?

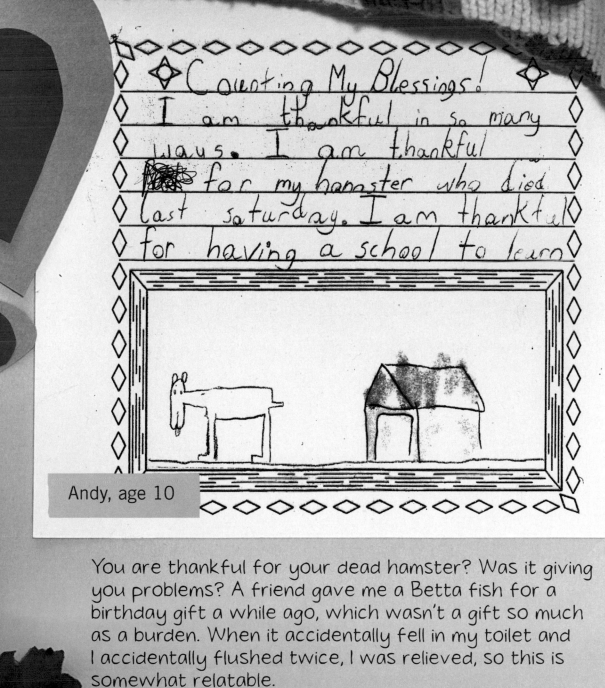

Counting My Blessings!

I am thankful in so many ways. I am thankful for my hamster who died last saturday. I am thankful for having a school to learn

Andy, age 10

You are thankful for your dead hamster? Was it giving you problems? A friend gave me a Betta fish for a birthday gift a while ago, which wasn't a gift so much as a burden. When it accidentally fell in my toilet and I accidentally flushed twice, I was relieved, so this is somewhat relatable.

F+

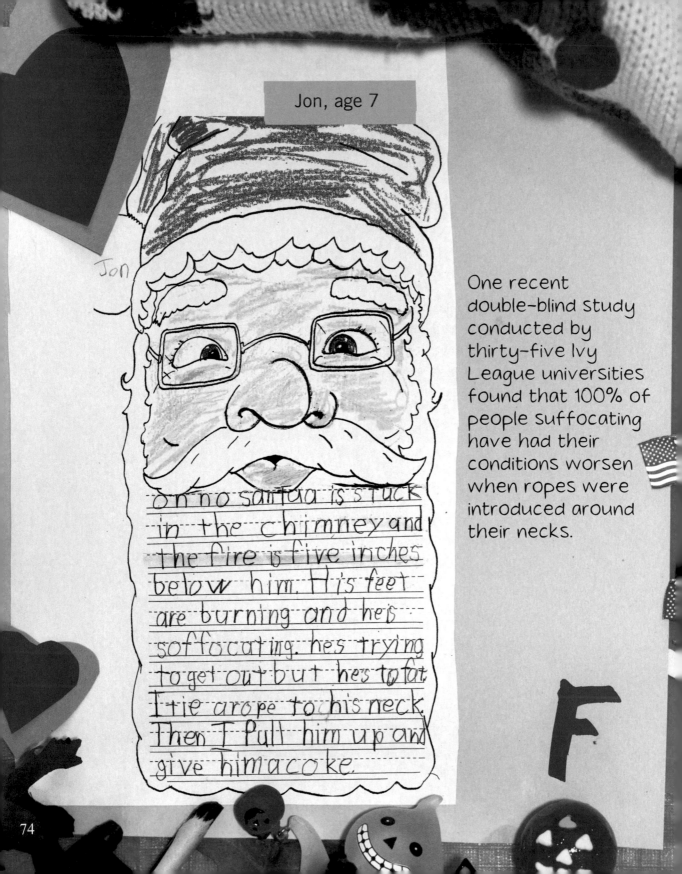

Jon, age 7

Jon

oh no santaa is stuck
in the chimney and
the fire is five inches
below him. His feet
are burning and hes
soffocating. hes trying
to get out but hes to fat.
I tie a rope to his neck.
Then I pull him up and
give him a coke.

One recent double-blind study conducted by thirty-five Ivy League universities found that 100% of people suffocating have had their conditions worsen when ropes were introduced around their necks.

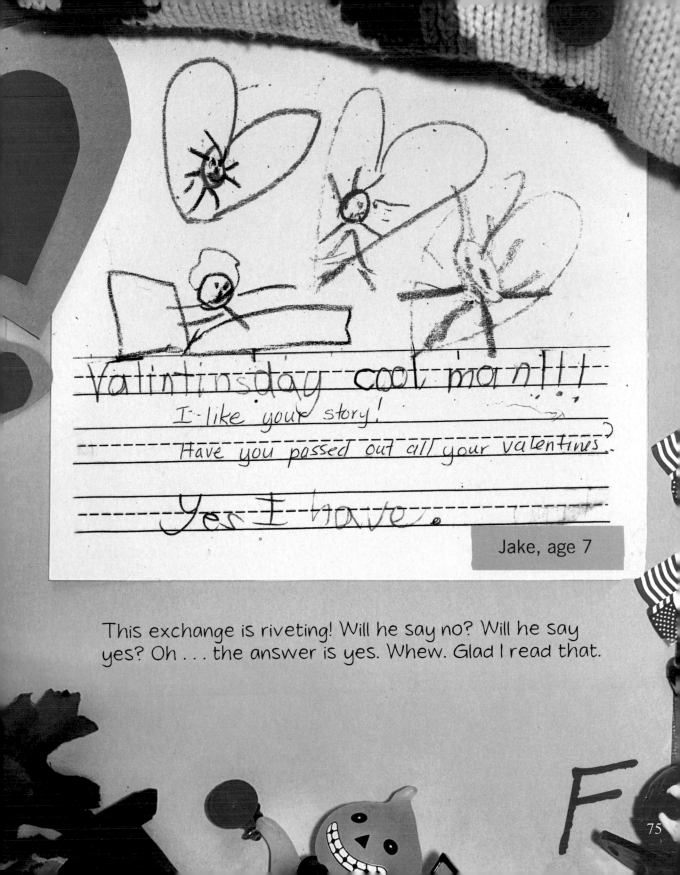

Valintinsday cool man!!!

I like your story!

Have you passed out all your valentines?

Yes I have.

Jake, age 7

This exchange is riveting! Will he say no? Will he say yes? Oh . . . the answer is yes. Whew. Glad I read that.

Drawing Your Family

Nicole, age 7

Wow, smug! Get over yourself already.

F

I wot a family to be wit' me and I wo family to love me so much.

Christian, age 5

my family is elegant.

No it isn't.

F

How are you this bad at everything? Spelling, writing, drawing basic shapes, grammar, and coloring inside the lines. All of it sucks.

F-

Pete, age 5

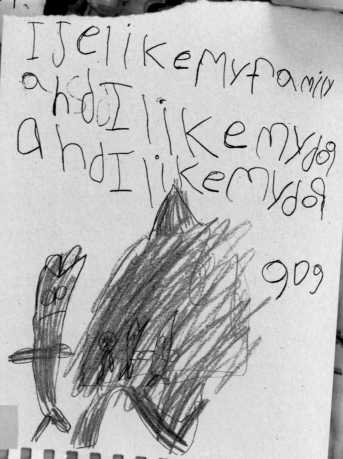

I JeliKeMyfamily
ahdI likeMydog
ahdI likeMydog

dog

Paige, age 5

On my most recent book tour, I signed someone's face with my crotch, and my signature was significantly more legible than this, Paige.

F

79

Let's see . . . oh this is nice, it's a nice family picture. Know what? I'll just go ahead and label them . . .

F

Bryon, age 6

Holly, age 4

Reported.

F

Amy, age 5

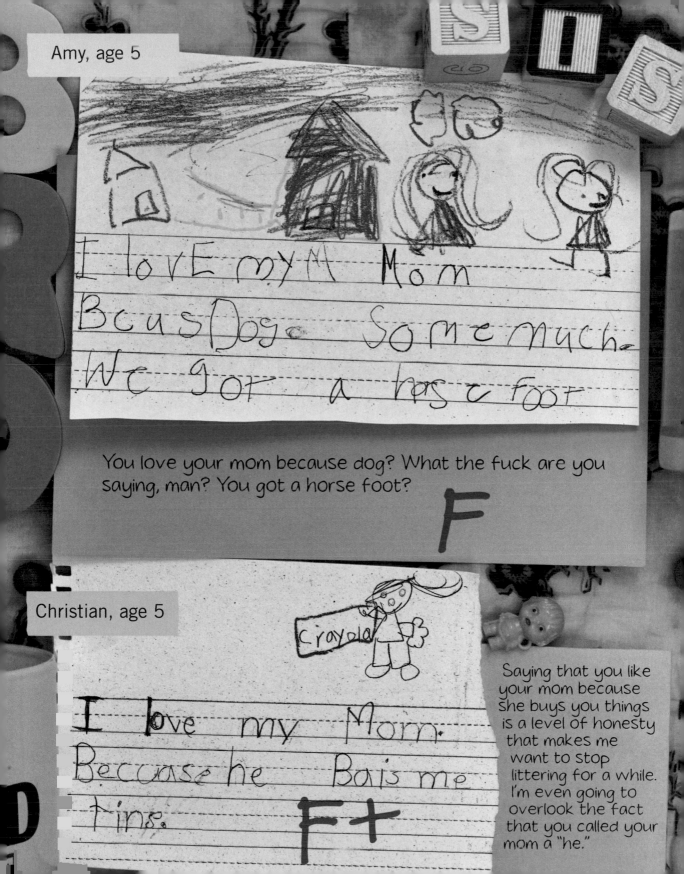

I loVE myM Mom
Bcus Dog. Some much.
We got a hos t foot

You love your mom because dog? What the fuck are you saying, man? You got a horse foot?

F

Christian, age 5

Crayola

I love my Mom.
Because he Bais me
tins. F+

Saying that you like your mom because she buys you things is a level of honesty that makes me want to stop littering for a while. I'm even going to overlook the fact that you called your mom a "he."

Look, Emily, I'm not going to sugarcoat this: your entire family is retarded. Everyone. Even the sun, by proximity.

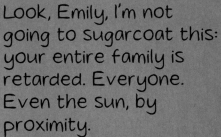

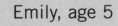
Emily, age 5

Brittany, age 4

Your family consists of your mom, your sister, you, and two floating heads. Why did you bother to turn this in?

F

82

Dwayne, age 4

Everyone in your family holds an apple and has a penis?

F

Zack, age 4

Your family is not this tall. Fuck you, liar.

F

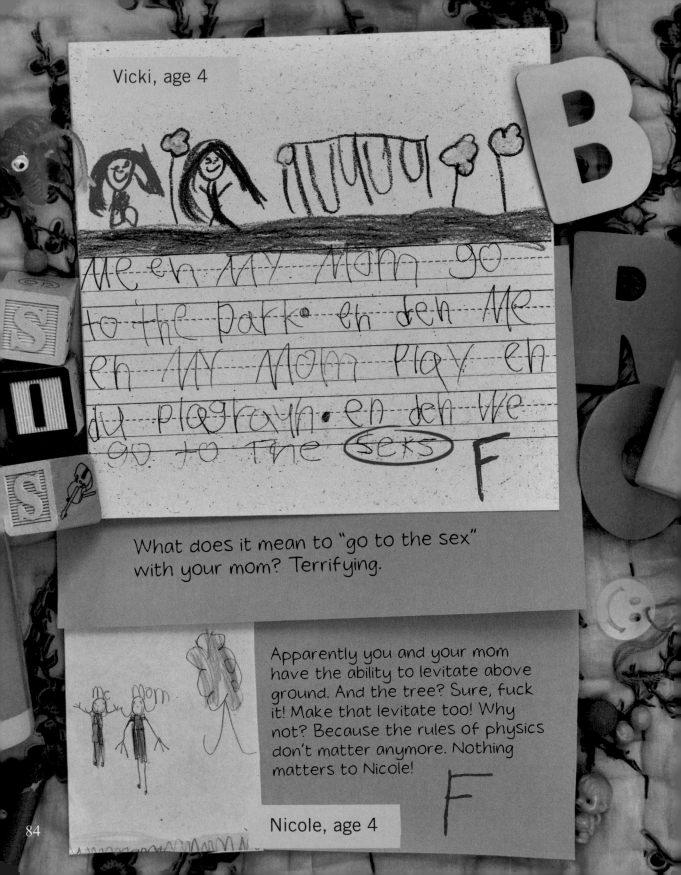

Vicki, age 4

Me en my mom go to the park. en den Me en my mom play en du playgrayn. en den we go to the seks

What does it mean to "go to the sex" with your mom? Terrifying.

Apparently you and your mom have the ability to levitate above ground. And the tree? Sure, fuck it! Make that levitate too! Why not? Because the rules of physics don't matter anymore. Nothing matters to Nicole!

Nicole, age 4

84

Nadi, age 5

What's mind-boggling about this is that Nadi drew every person in her family as almost identical, labeled herself on the left, and then decided that for some reason the nearly identical one on the right more accurately represented her. So she crossed out the original and relabeled herself on the right instead.

F

Matty, age 5

Your mom is teetering dangerously in a giant chair and all you can think about is your pancakes. You are a hateful child.

F

When me and my mom macK pancaks Ferst We put Kereehi Next We Back it ethen We eat it!

Jared, age 4

A B d d e F G U I I
H I I K L N N W
P o S T U X Y Z

You were assigned to write a story about your family. You wrote the alphabet. Not only is the alphabet not a story, but you wrote the sequence wrong.

F

86

Ashley, age 6

My family

12 Mom

6 yores old

F

You know when you see a homeless person walking around wearing fishnet stockings, a wig, and some random sporting equipment, and you start to smirk before you realize he's mentally handicapped and you're an asshole? This drawing personifies that feeling. At first you see the parents, ages thirty-seven and twelve, wearing heels and you start to smirk. Then you realize the girl who drew it has a unibrow and stumps for feet, and you feel like a dick. Emphasis on you, and not me, since looking at a couple thousand of these hardens you, and you stop feeling anything at all.

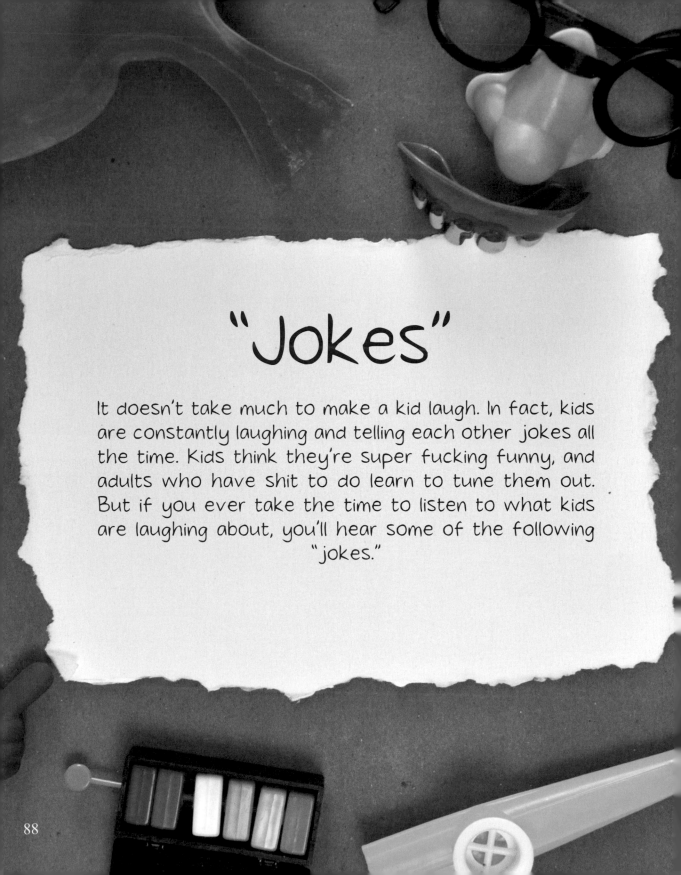

"Jokes"

It doesn't take much to make a kid laugh. In fact, kids are constantly laughing and telling each other jokes all the time. Kids think they're super fucking funny, and adults who have shit to do learn to tune them out. But if you ever take the time to listen to what kids are laughing about, you'll hear some of the following "jokes."

Pam, age 10

what do you call a sleeping bull

Answer

a bull dozer

F

I told this joke to a hot brunette in a bar one night, and she thought it was so funny she gave me her number and told me to call her anytime I wanted her to gobble my meat wrench. She used those exact words.

Violet, age 11

F F F F
F Runaway F
   Pencil!!!!

This is why kids get thrown out windows sometimes.

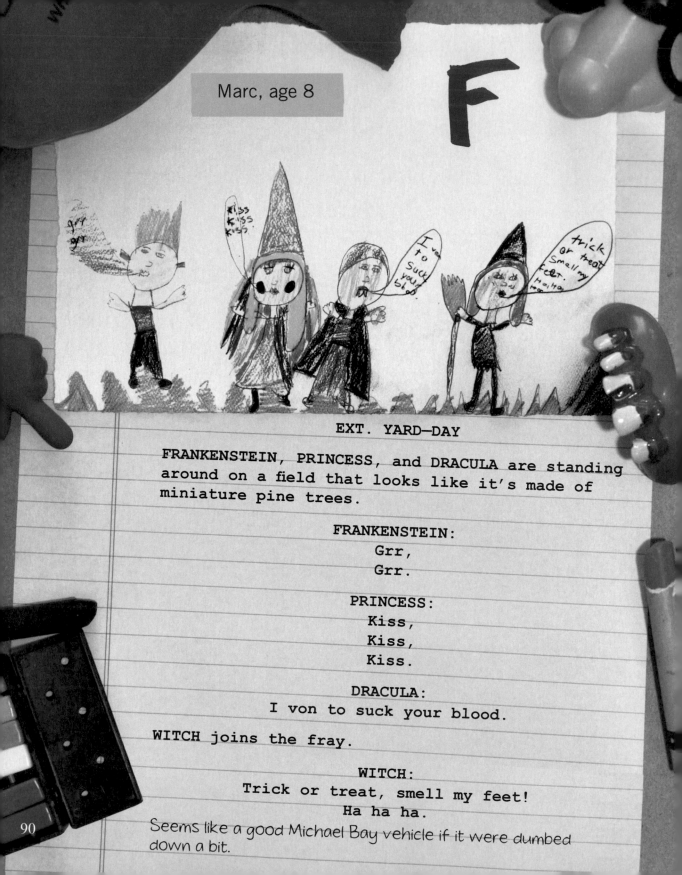

EXT. YARD—DAY

FRANKENSTEIN, PRINCESS, and DRACULA are standing around on a field that looks like it's made of miniature pine trees.

                    FRANKENSTEIN:
                        Grr,
                        Grr.

                    PRINCESS:
                        Kiss,
                        Kiss,
                        Kiss.

                    DRACULA:
            I von to suck your blood.

WITCH joins the fray.

                    WITCH:
        Trick or treat, smell my feet!
                    Ha ha ha.

Seems like a good Michael Bay vehicle if it were dumbed down a bit.

Today I see a snak and snak bit mos but :! hahaha hahaha

This not only isn't a joke, it's not even a story, or a sentence. It's not even what most people would consider a thought.

F+

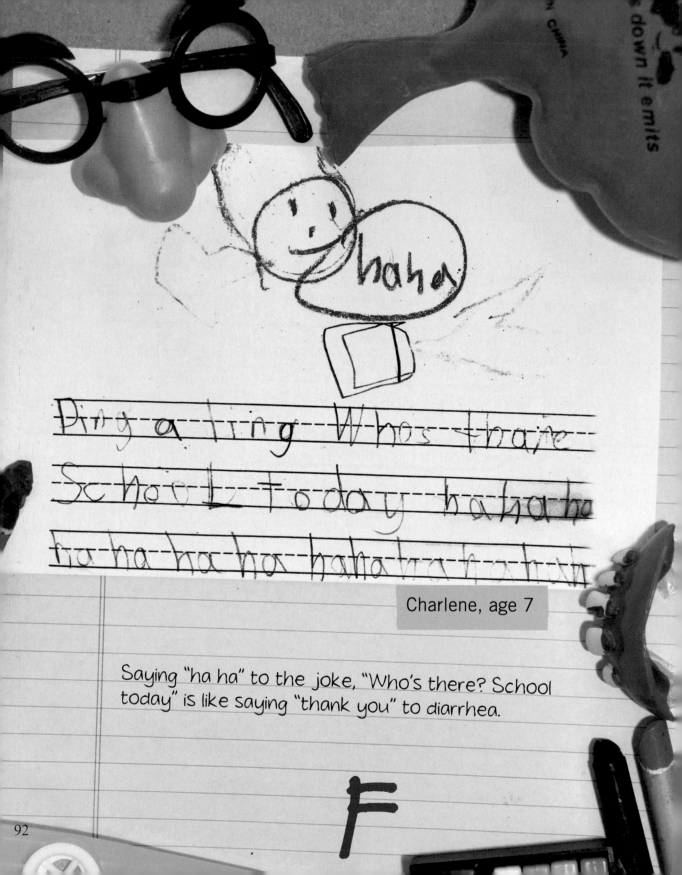

haha

Ding a ling Whos thare
Schoot today ha ha ha
ha ha ha ha hahaha ta hah

Charlene, age 7

Saying "ha ha" to the joke, "Who's there? School today" is like saying "thank you" to diarrhea.

F

Shitty Inventions

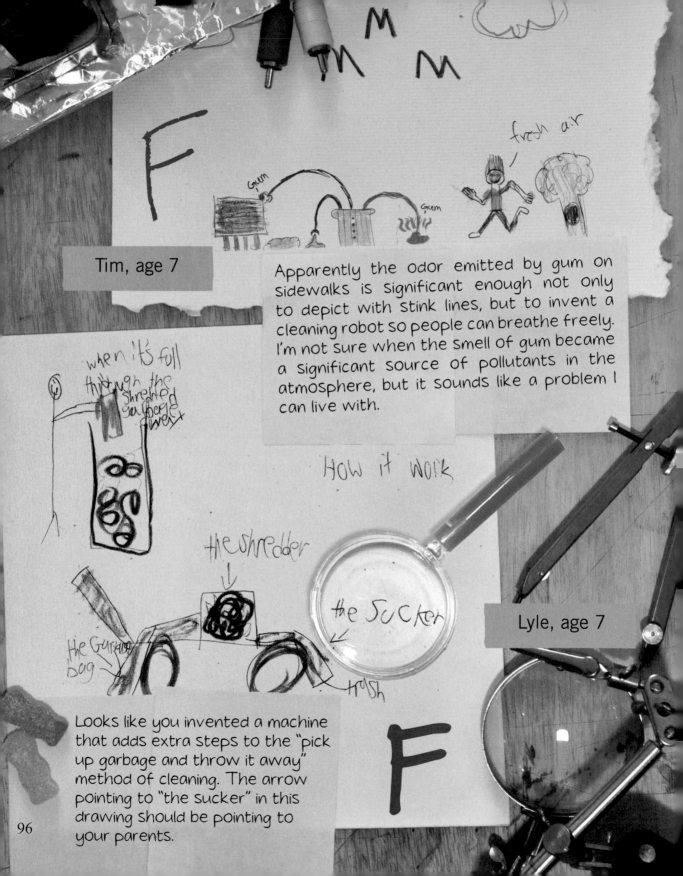

M M M M

F

Gum

Gum

fresh air

Tim, age 7

Apparently the odor emitted by gum on sidewalks is significant enough not only to depict with stink lines, but to invent a cleaning robot so people can breathe freely. I'm not sure when the smell of gum became a significant source of pollutants in the atmosphere, but it sounds like a problem I can live with.

when it's full
through the
shredded
garbage
chest

How it work

the shredder

the Garbage
bag

the sucker

trash

Lyle, age 7

Looks like you invented a machine that adds extra steps to the "pick up garbage and throw it away" method of cleaning. The arrow pointing to "the sucker" in this drawing should be pointing to your parents.

F

Sean, age 8

A giant "cleaning" robot with soap-laser beams, broom arms, and dust-cleaner eyes? Good job, I'll take two.

97

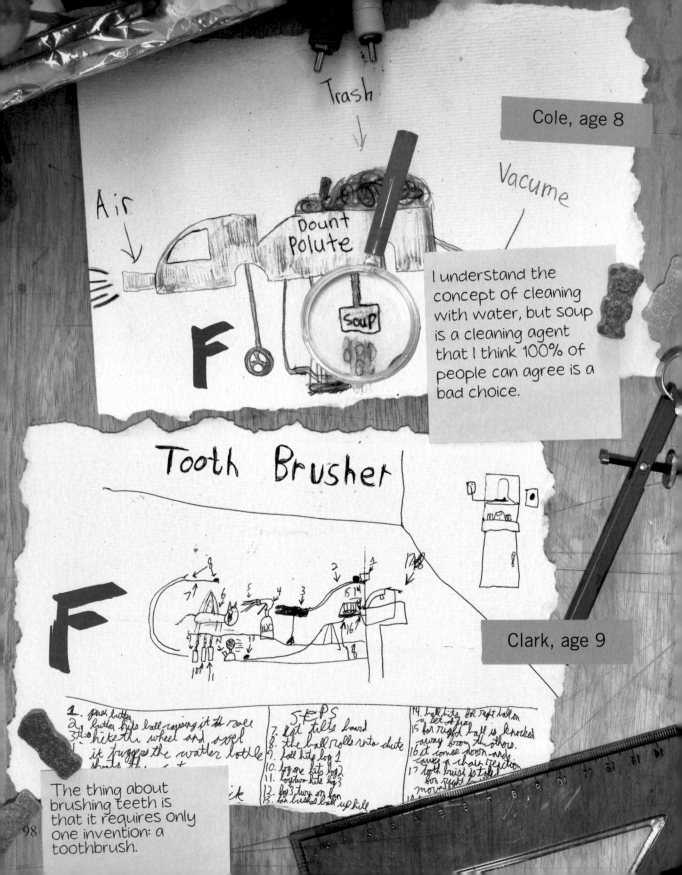

Trash

Vacume

Air

Dount Polute

F

Soup

I understand the concept of cleaning with water, but soup is a cleaning agent that I think 100% of people can agree is a bad choice.

Tooth Brusher

F

1. *push button*
2. *butta hits ball raising it the rail*
3. *tho hike the wheel and axel*
   it triggers the watter bottle

STEPS
7. *bat tilts board*
8. *the ball rolls into chute*
9. *ball hits log 1*
10. *log one hits log 2*
11. *log two hits log 3*
12. *log 3 turns on fan*
13. *fan pushes ball up hill*

14. *ball hits bar right ball on*
    to set of fire
15. *for right ball is knocked*
    away from the other
16. *it comes down and*
    cause of chain reaction
17. *tooth brush is told*
    for Right b...

The thing about brushing teeth is that it requires only one invention: a toothbrush.

Samuel, age 6

Samuel was asked to draw the solution to the Arab/ Israeli conflict. This is what he drew: an airboat armed with penguin missiles and camouflaged in Rastafari colors. Airboats are meant to go on marshy swamps and shallow water. So in other words, neither Palestine nor Israel. Though if this were a metaphor for the mire that the peace process is stuck in, this drawing is borderline brilliant. But it's not, so, *F*.

A lion toothbrush with toothpaest

green goo

Garrik, age 7

Did you bother to think about what evolutionary purpose having two mouths would serve? There's a reason there aren't any creatures on earth with two mouths, and you won't find any in space either.

F

Ethan, age 7

Next time you draw the Statue of Liberty, try not to make her look so conniving. She's holding the torch, not trying to sneak off with it, traitor.

F

Cool Tree

Melissa, age 15

"What's up, Candy-house? 'Sup, black sun? Who me? I'm just the coolest fucking tree in the universe. I'm just going to sit here and chill, cool as fuck." I'd buy this tree a beer if he didn't already get his drinks comp'd at every bar in the city. He picks karaoke songs that bring the house down every time. He wears weird plaid shirts and clashing patterns, but rather than sticking out, he just looks cooler and sets new trends. He drinks a gin and tonic with two limes and doesn't give a fuck if that was your drink in college. It's his drink now, you dig?

Nate, age 15

Cool tree says: "Pussy."

please dont cuss at me

F

"What do you mean the kids at school still bully you? Did you ask them to stop? You did? Well did you try saying please?" How's that polite thing working out for you, Nate? I was never a bully in school, but you're so dorky that even I want to slap you in your nerd mouth.

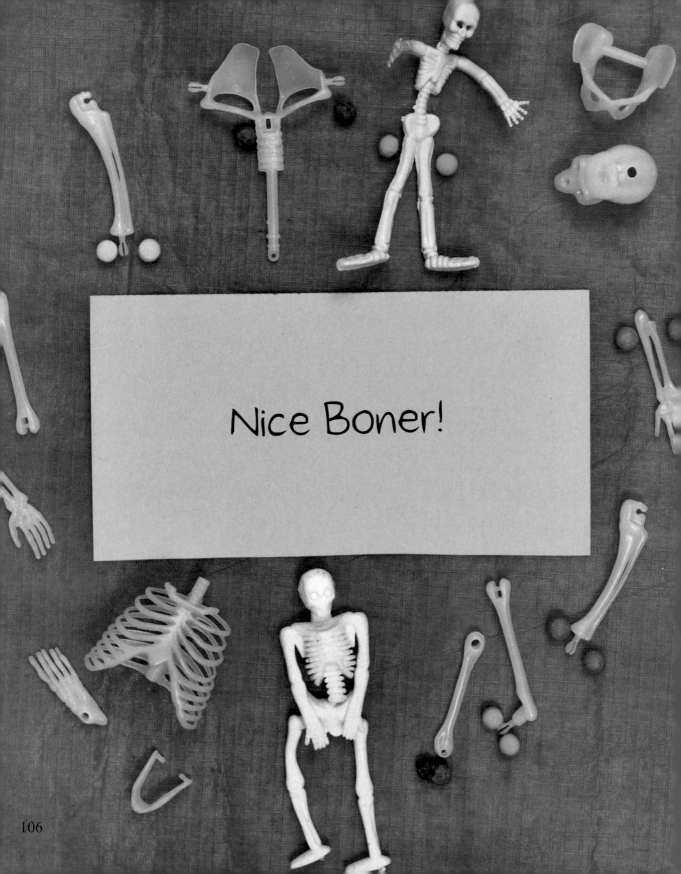

Nice Boner!

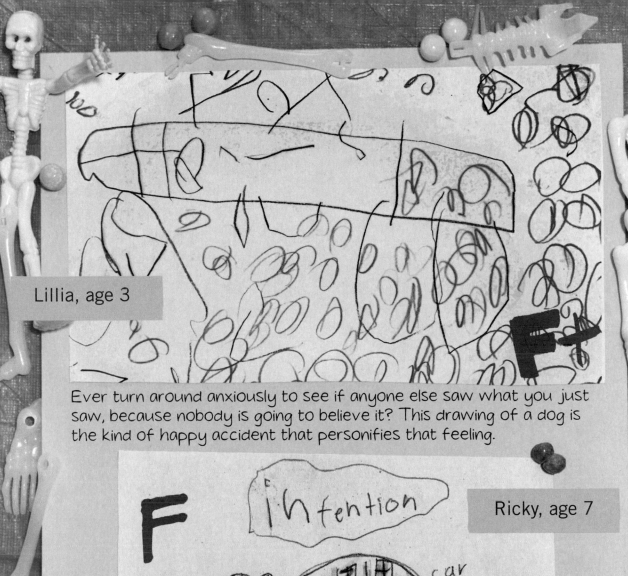

Lillia, age 3

Ever turn around anxiously to see if anyone else saw what you just saw, because nobody is going to believe it? This drawing of a dog is the kind of happy accident that personifies that feeling.

Ricky, age 7

When you draw a car that looks this phallic, being a five-year-old child affords you certain privileges that adults wouldn't get. For example, people might give you the benefit of the doubt and think it wasn't your intention. But when you write the word "intention" above your car, and draw a giant spiky dong on one end of it, you can't play the innocence card anymore.

My hero

←Chichero
Hernandez

← Soccer
Player

Joscar, age 7

"Number 9, please put your tiny dick away."

F

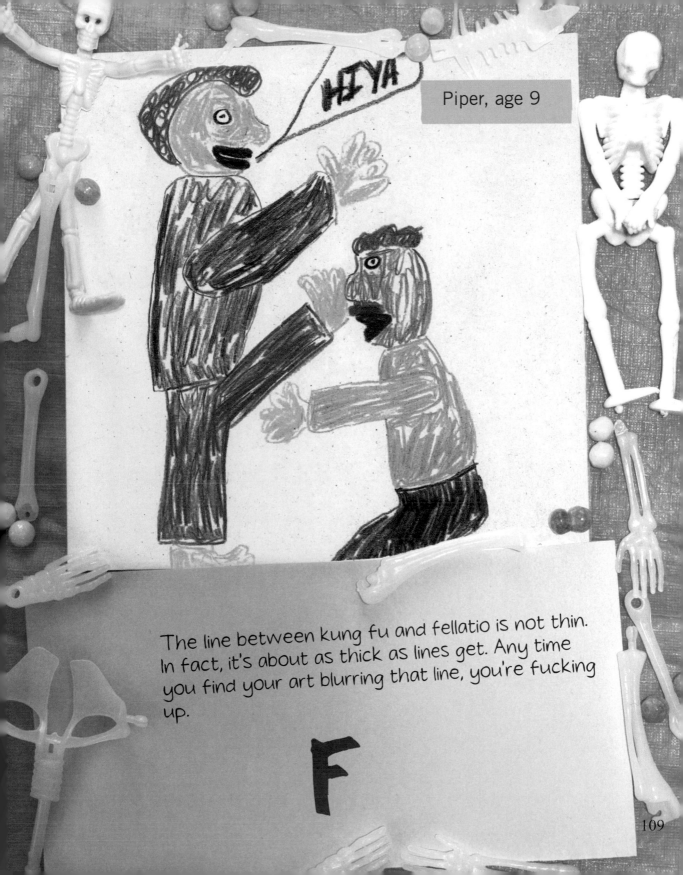

Piper, age 9

The line between kung fu and fellatio is not thin. In fact, it's about as thick as lines get. Any time you find your art blurring that line, you're fucking up.

F

109

Dom, age 7

F

eats people

Ploto

I'm not sure what's more disconcerting: the machine that eats people, the hook penis on the alien, or the fact that fast-food dollar menus have spared people like you from natural selection.

F+

Abraham, age 5

If your dog ever gets uppity and starts wearing a top hat, show him who's master by balancing on his back with your obscenely large penis.

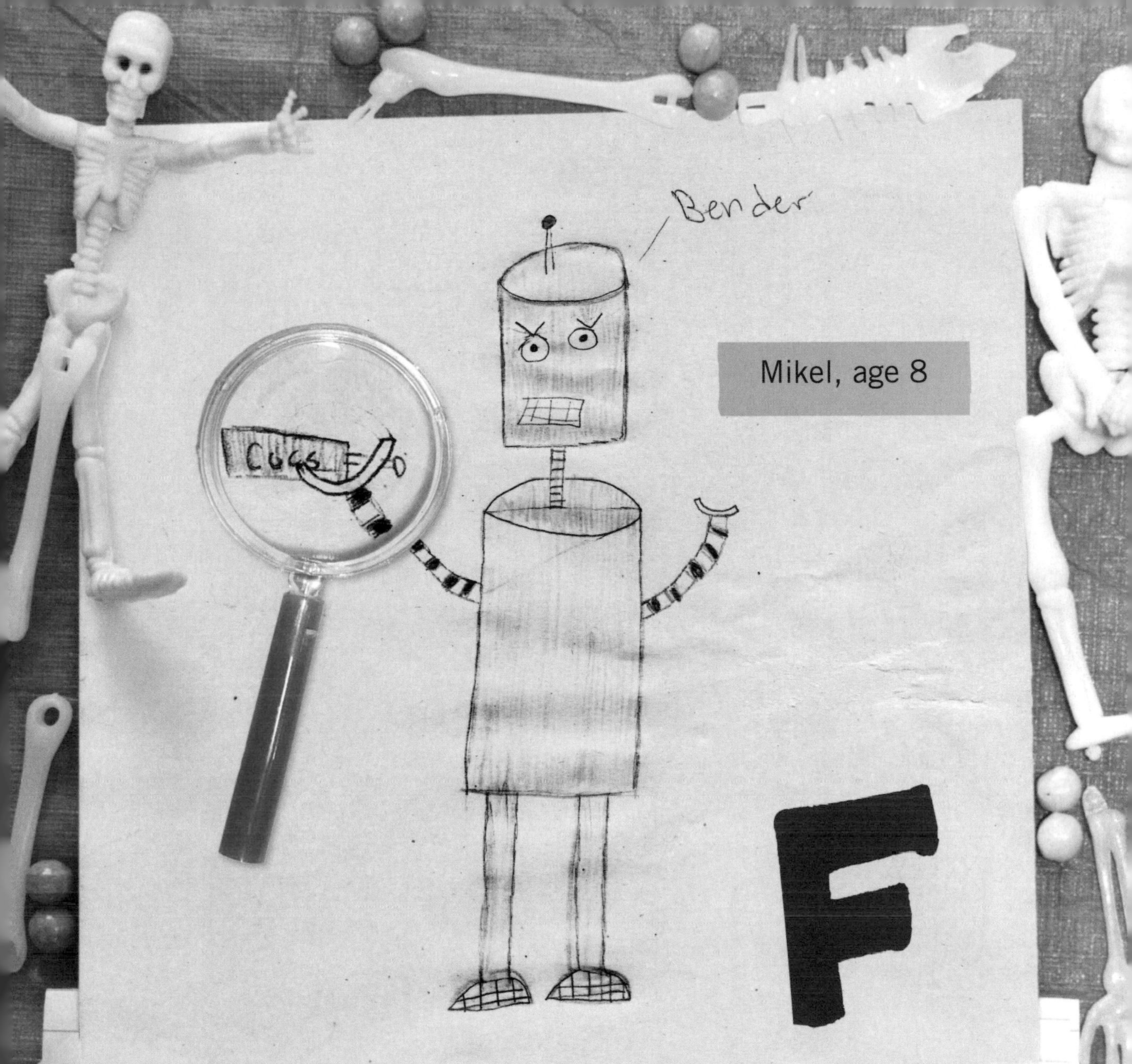

Bender

Mikel, age 8

In the future, we'll all have our own
personal robots to handle the laborious
chore of carrying our cocks.

Cameron, age 7

F+

Super Sragnth

Finally, a superhero whose power rivals my own. Next time, do a better job erasing.

Laurence, age 10

F

"The good news is, we got a permit to construct the world's largest cookie. The bad news is, we can only use dildos."

ThiR Ra horse

Alan, age 4

F

Are you fucking with me?

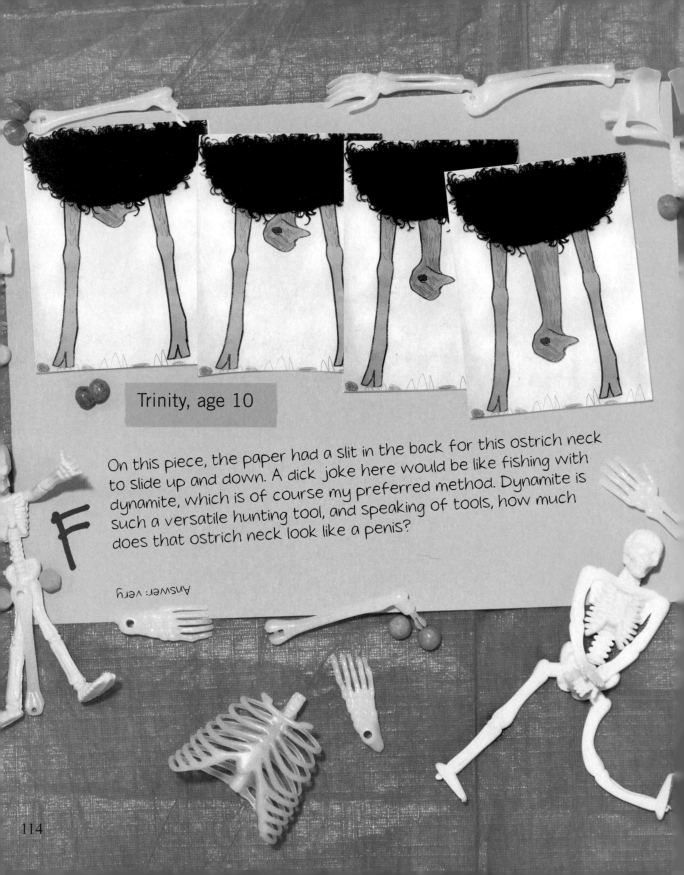

Trinity, age 10

On this piece, the paper had a slit in the back for this ostrich neck to slide up and down. A dick joke here would be like fishing with dynamite, which is of course my preferred method. Dynamite is such a versatile hunting tool, and speaking of tools, how much does that ostrich neck look like a penis?

F

Answer: very

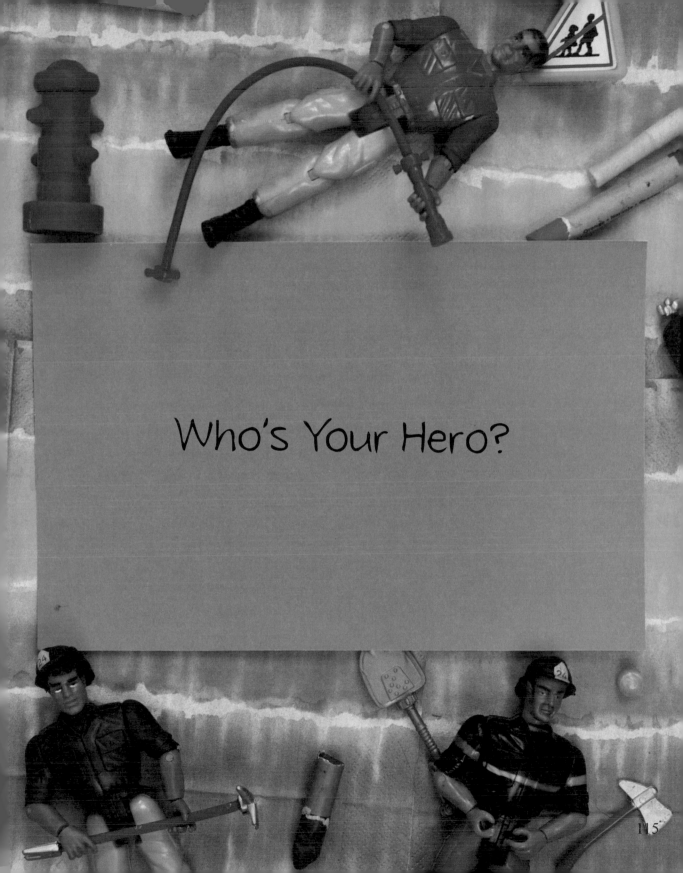

Who's Your Hero?

115

my teddy bear!

Your hero is a teddy bear with one eye pulled out that you keep on a pink bed? I feel like this is the beginning of an urban legend. Here's a spoiler, Bryce: you're going to have one of your hands replaced with a hook someday. You will come across a parked car, and just when you go to open the door, the car will speed away, tearing the hook from your arm.

F.

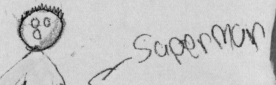

Saperman

Saperman: superhero by day, mild-mannered bowling ball by night.

F

Well, he is the Son of God, and he did turn water into wine, so I guess standing on a cloud while balancing a plate on his head is no biggie.

F+

Jesus

Katy, age 6

117

Wow, your dog sure is brave when the pit bull is behind a fence.

My Dog Saving me from a Pitbull.

Dorie, age 6

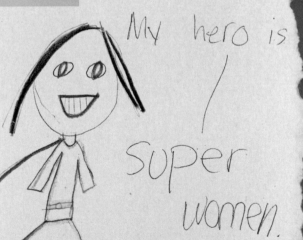
My hero is super women.

I guess if I were deaf, a woman with no hands would be more than perfect—she'd be super.

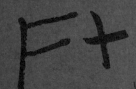

If ninja turtles always looked this sad, they would have canceled the show halfway through the opening credits.

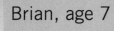
Brian, age 7

F

Edgar, age 8

Although Sonic is not a New York cabbie like you've drawn him here, I kinda wish he were. I even like his catch phrase: "ok."

F+

Beowulf Hero Essay

My mom is a very brave woman. She is thoughtful, kind, and thinks before saying or doing anything. My mom realizes that for every action, there's a reaction. This makes her an excellent strategizer, which is a fine trait in a hero. My mom is constantly using psychology - or reversed psychology to get me to do things. She could therefore beat Grendel and his mother very easily, just like Beowulf did. Actually, my mom is a lot like Beowulf. She is powerful, respected, and loved.

So what is the answer to the question, "What is a hero?" There really is no right or wrong answer, except for the fact that a hero isn't just muscles andsmiles. A true hero is full of heart and full of life.

No, your mom isn't powerful enough to destroy Grendel, even if she uses "reversed" psychology. Here's how that exchange would go down:

Maddox, age 32

F

120

My mom and Dad is my hero they help me in saff I need help In

Apparently not grammar.

Margaret, age 8

121

My hero is a baled eagle

Shannon, age 8

You know what, Shannon? Your "baled eagle" is a masterpiece. Let's go ahead and put it on the U.S. quarter!

This could happen, Shannon! Either that or you will major in business administration, get knocked up young, and never leave your hometown. Anything is possible!

F

UNITED STATES OF AMERICA

BALED EAGLE

IN GOD WE TRUST

S

QUARTER DOLLAR

Hey, Emily, what color do you think the Green Lantern should be? Here's a hint: it's the first word in his name. Here's another hint: you highlighted it. Give up? It's the color of this letter: **F**

Emily, age 7

SPIDERMAN

Brent, age 6

Even seemingly simple tasks like posing as a newspaper photographer would be nontrivial with giant wooden arms and claws for hands. Forget the superhero story, I could watch an entire movie just about a guy trying to do things like tie his shoes or make coffee with arms like that.

F+

Space   Godzlue   vs.   Sowpremon

wate!

Luke, age 7

"Oh no! Space Godzlue is barfing on the
Washington Monument! This looks like a job
for . . . Sowpremon!"

F

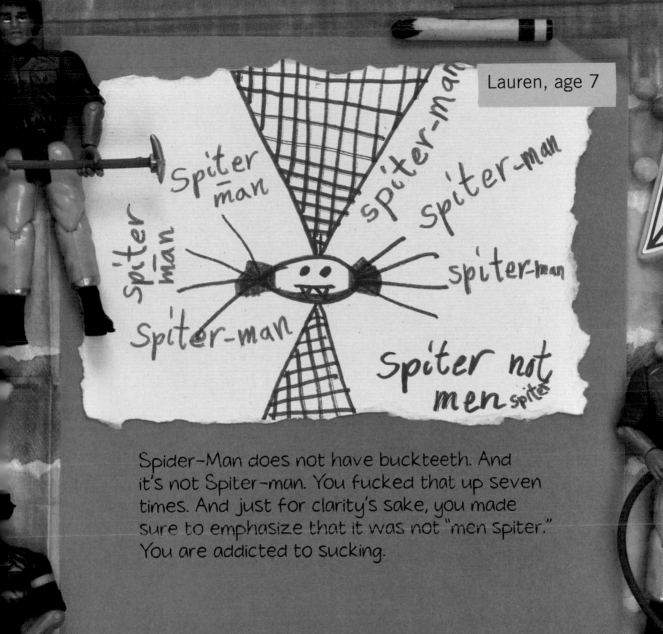

Spider–Man does not have buckteeth. And it's not Spiter-man. You fucked that up seven times. And just for clarity's sake, you made sure to emphasize that it was not "men spiter." You are addicted to sucking.

F

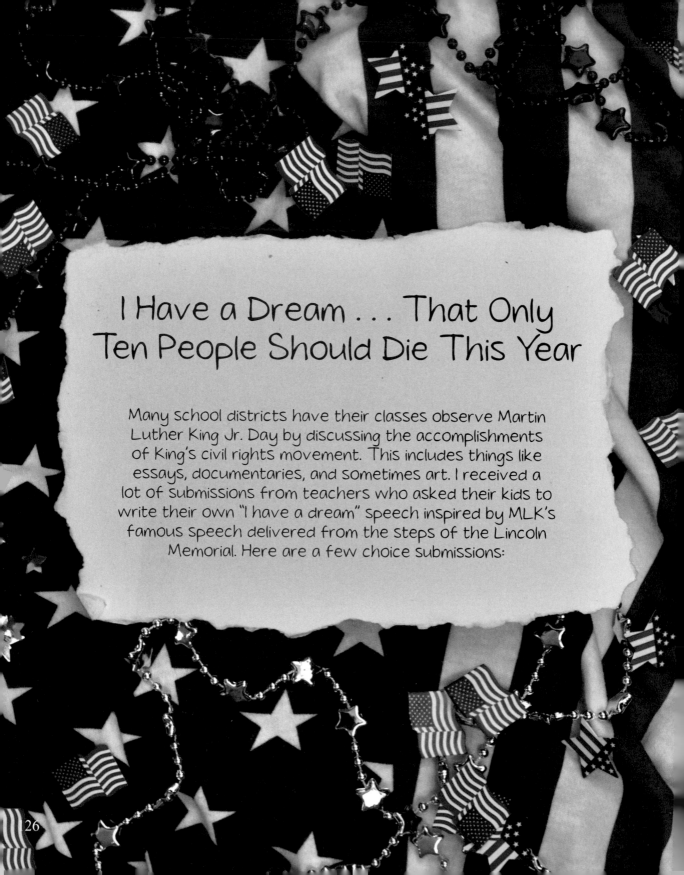

I Have a Dream . . . That Only Ten People Should Die This Year

Many school districts have their classes observe Martin Luther King Jr. Day by discussing the accomplishments of King's civil rights movement. This includes things like essays, documentaries, and sometimes art. I received a lot of submissions from teachers who asked their kids to write their own "I have a dream" speech inspired by MLK's famous speech delivered from the steps of the Lincoln Memorial. Here are a few choice submissions:

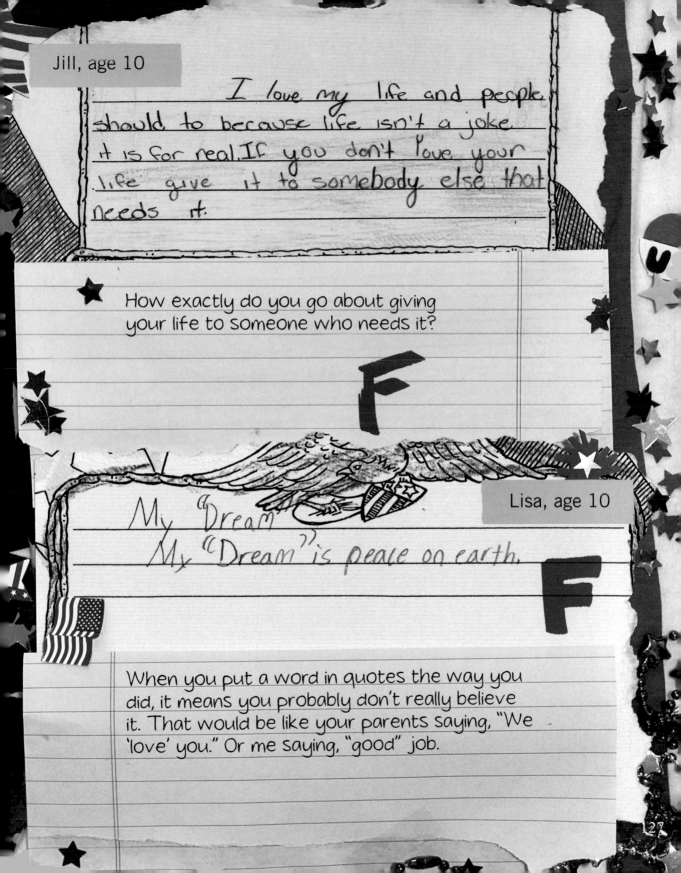

Jill, age 10

I love my life and people should to because life isn't a joke. It is for real. If you don't love your life give it to somebody else that needs it.

How exactly do you go about giving your life to someone who needs it?

F

Lisa, age 10

My "Dream"
My "Dream" is peace on earth.

F

When you put a word in quotes the way you did, it means you probably don't really believe it. That would be like your parents saying, "We 'love' you." Or me saying, "good" job.

"I had a dream"

I had a dream that my grandma and my mom were fighting. Only because I didn't want to go food-4-less to buy food to cook.

Simone, age 10

It's supposed to be "I have a dream," as in a hope or a vision for the future. Not "I had a dream," as in the literal dream you had a few nights ago.

F

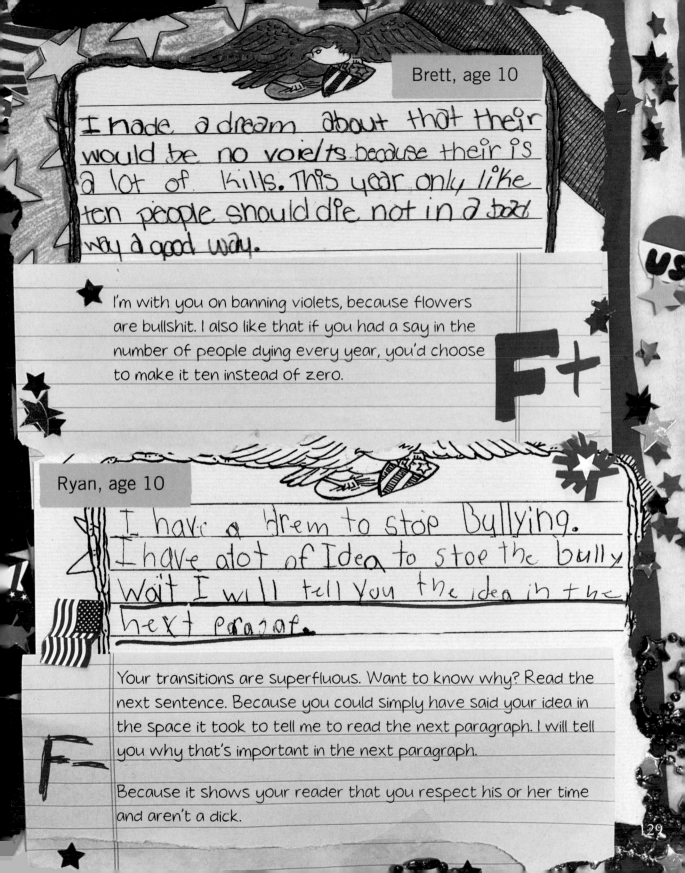

Brett, age 10

I hade a dream about that their would be no voielts because their is a lot of kills. This year only like ten people should die not in a bad way a good way.

I'm with you on banning violets, because flowers are bullshit. I also like that if you had a say in the number of people dying every year, you'd choose to make it ten instead of zero.

F+

Ryan, age 10

I have a drem to stop Bullying. I have alot of Idea to stop the bully Wait I will tell you the idea in the next parajaf.

F-

Your transitions are superfluous. Want to know why? Read the next sentence. Because you could simply have said your idea in the space it took to tell me to read the next paragraph. I will tell you why that's important in the next paragraph.

Because it shows your reader that you respect his or her time and aren't a dick.

29

I have a dream of that military gets more training. If we dont give them that much training The Spetznas will attack L.A. We must defend ouselves from Afghanistan. Its a nightmare to the Army. We need lots of protection.

Alot of wars was to protect California. If we lose we might be slaves. They will tacce our home We will have to join the military. I hope this will happen.

Al, age 10

F

USA

You are correct in that almost none of our budget goes toward training the military to protect Los Angeles from "Spetsnaz," the Russian special forces units that defend the Russian Ministry of Internal Affairs. The only war that was fought exclusively to protect California was the Mexican-American War, and they were fighting to protect California from the Americans.

F+

My dream is to keep the world from harmony. Harmony that might hurt peoples life and the world. The world and our life is like a precious daisy. Without them there is nothing, nothing at all.

Hillary, age 10

I share your dream of keeping the world from harmony. Join me, Hillary:

My dream is to be a ~~peple~~ Police. Because they can get alot of money.

They can Park the car how ever they want.

Benny, age 10

Hey, fuckface, cops aren't supposed to park their cars however they want. I know you think being a cop gives you special privileges, but parking in the red zone when you aren't responding to an emergency makes you look like an asshole.

F-

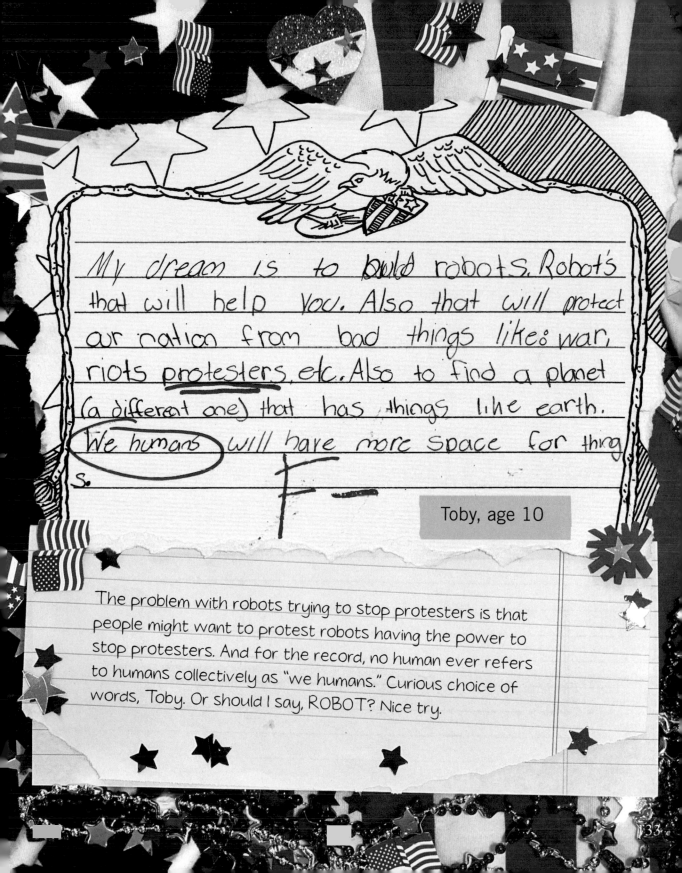

My dream is to build robots. Robot's that will help you. Also that will protect our nation from bad things like: war, riots protesters, etc. Also to find a planet (a different one) that has things like earth. We humans will have more space for things.

F-

Toby, age 10

The problem with robots trying to stop protesters is that people might want to protest robots having the power to stop protesters. And for the record, no human ever refers to humans collectively as "we humans." Curious choice of words, Toby. Or should I say, ROBOT? Nice try.

133

Drawings of Teachers and Parents

Troy, age 9

I'm sure your teacher appreciates your drawing her like a transvestite hooker.

F

Nicholas, age 6

Well, you got Mrs. Kemp's gender wrong. But I can't fault you too much, because you accidentally drew the late Gregory Peck.

F+

Mrs. Kemp

Rendel, age 5

Mom

You know those tears of joy a mother has when her child makes a gift for her? Sometimes they're tears of sorrow.

Steve, age 9

my dad look like this →

I haven't met your dad, but I know he doesn't look like this. I've never been more sure of anything in my life.

F+

This is a Marie.
これは、マリーです。

This whole everything-from-
Japan-is-weird-or-cute-or-tentacle-rape
thing is starting to make sense. This works on
so many levels, and some I'm not even cognizant
of yet.

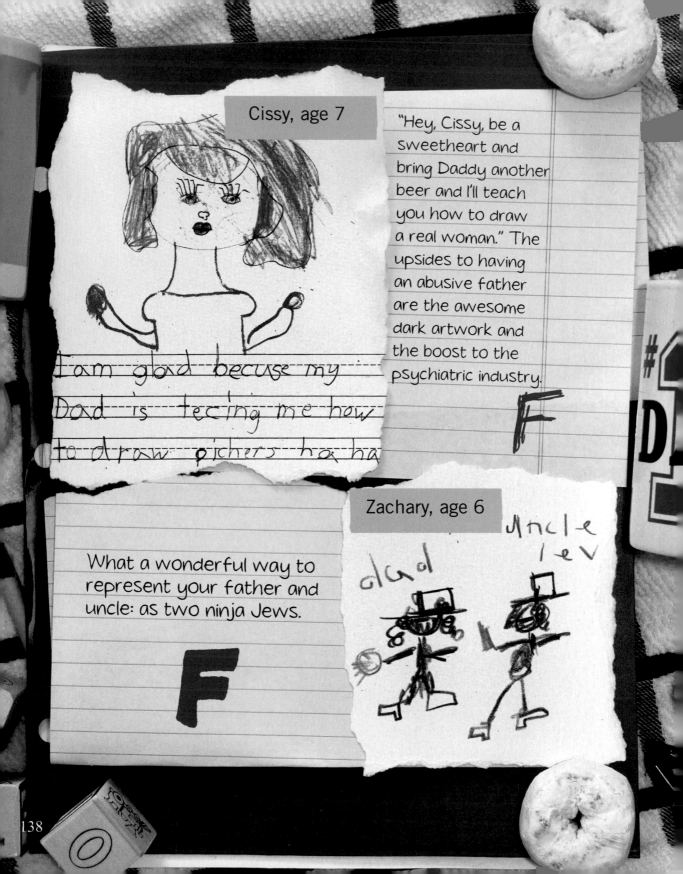

Cissy, age 7

"Hey, Cissy, be a sweetheart and bring Daddy another beer and I'll teach you how to draw a real woman." The upsides to having an abusive father are the awesome dark artwork and the boost to the psychiatric industry.

F

I am glad becuse my Dad is tecing me how to draw pichers ha ha

Zachary, age 6

dad   Uncle lev

What a wonderful way to represent your father and uncle: as two ninja Jews.

F

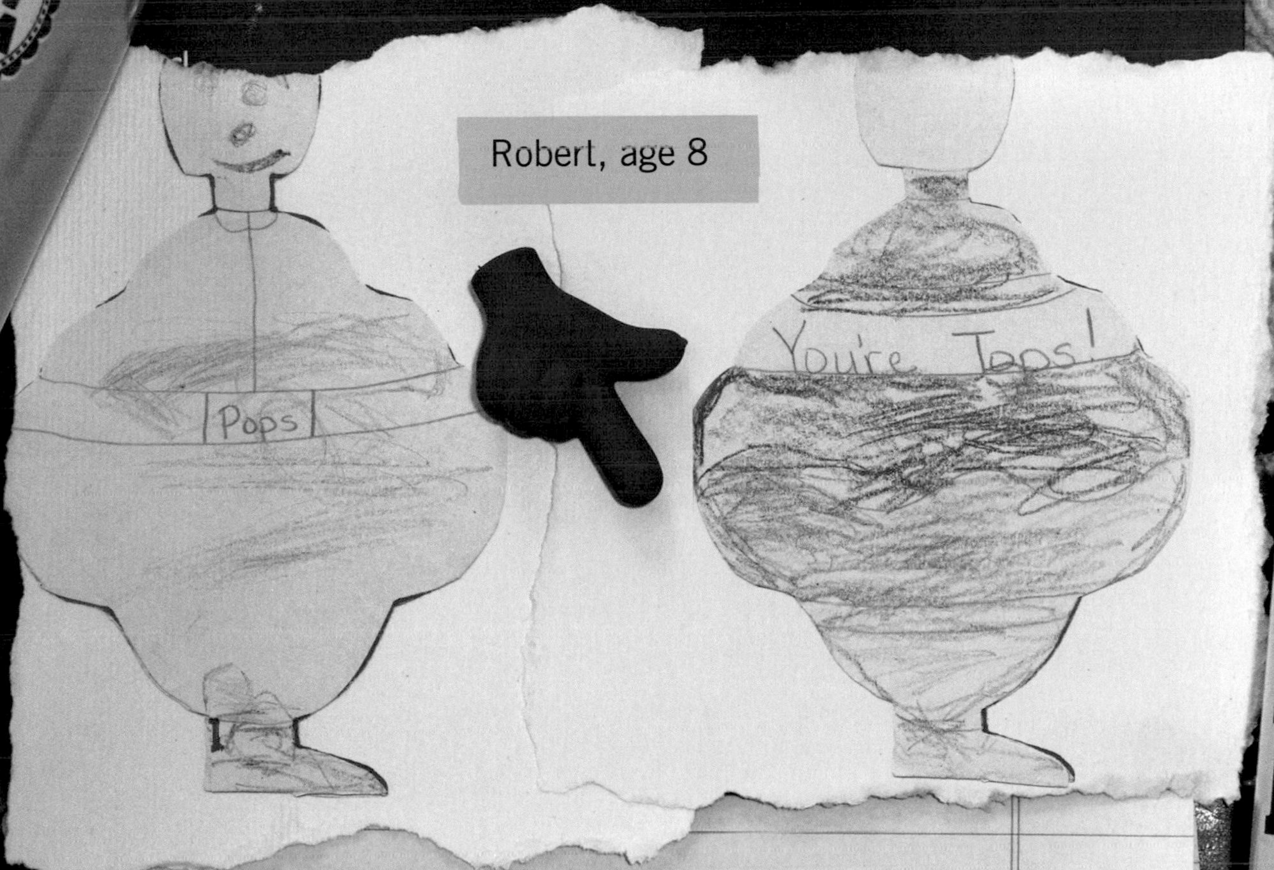

Robert, age 8

Pops

You're Tops!

Why not just get a job and buy him something he might actually like instead? Giving is easy. Here, I'll start:

Surprise!

If I received this gift for my retirement, I'd spend a long, lonely night with a gun in my mouth reflecting on my life.

F−

Things That Scare You

F

Oh no! Look out: it's a big pink shark! The biggest threat this shark would pose is the cleaning bill to wash the skid marks from my underwear from laughing so hard.

Alexis, age 9

Maybe instead of zombies, you should be worried about early onset diabetes, because with a name like "Ascheyleighe," your parents can't be making too many other smart choices concerning your upbringing.

F

Ascheyleighe, age 9

Something that scares me is... Standing at the edge of the cliff

Trevor, age 9

ahhhhhhh!

~Shark

Who wouldn't be afraid of falling off a cliff and into the mouth of a waiting shark? Oh, yeah, everybody. That's because it has never happened throughout the entire course of human history.

F-

F-

Vampiers

This got me thinking about the possibility of a vampire becoming obese by feeding on fat people, which is a poignant commentary about obesity in America. I wondered if it was intentional until I noticed the spelling of "vampiers."

Rachel, age 10

I'M SCARED;
MY MOM

Well, I have to admit, Candice, your mom looks like a total bitch.

Candice, age 9

F+

KidNap!

Roger, age 6

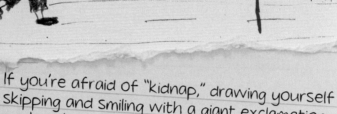

F

If you're afraid of "kidnap," drawing yourself skipping and smiling with a giant exclamation mark isn't the most effective way of conveying fear. You actually look pretty stoked about "Kidnap!"

Rob, age 8

F

I almost don't have to grade this because he looks like he's giving himself an F. But just for good measure: F

I'm scared of turanchelas. I can't see a house spider or I will scream to death!!!

Annie, age 10

F

ahhh!!!!

How do you know you'll scream to death if you see a house spider? Has it happened before? No, because you'd be dead.

BBBBBBBBZZZZZZZZ

daaaahmm!!

I'm scared of Beesbb

Bee

Katy, age 8

I'm not just scared of Bees but, their stingers!

I Freak out when theres bees around me!

F

What's puzzling about this is that you draw the distinction between the bees and their stingers. You realize that a bee poses no threat to you without a stinger, right? No, of course not. You are eight years old and don't know anything.

Romald from mc donals

Agreed.
Terrifying.

F

Lana, age 8

Maybe more terrifying than stupid because it has a human face. But maybe more stupid than terrifying because it has a double chin. I can't decide.

F

Zombies in love? Where are their Affliction T-shirts? Heyo!

F

Shoshanna, age 7

coyote

traffic

Kelly, age 8

You realize that the probability of being chased by a coyote on any given day is pretty close to zero, and that the probability of a road being built directly into a cliff is actually zero, right? Life is not a Road Runner cartoon.

F

Jason, age 8

I aim scared of Hicks

F

Window

Big Buildings

The great North American Hick; known to dwell atop the highest urban skyscrapers. And ah yes, windows. Thank you for labeling them.

This is how I look when I feel <u>scared</u>:

I feel scared when: I see scared movies.

Some people hide or cower when they're scared. You grow tits on your face.

F

Dear Teacher, I'm Sorry You Wasted Your Time

When kids misbehave in class, a lot of teachers, parents, and substitutes have them write apology letters. Here are the best of the worst:

I appreaciate that you waste your time to come here and teech us I appreaciate that you are here to take care of us when Ms.kemp isn't here. You are the best subtitute we have and I appreciate that.

Betsie, age 10

You probably meant to say "spend" instead of "waste" when writing your apology letter, but waste actually works better.

F+

MRS. SWANSON,
I hope you are good in Bed
Josie

Josie, age 10

This is the best addition to a get well card I've ever seen.

F+

155

Dear Miss Lee,

I am so sorry for disrespecting you. I feel
really disapointed I promise that will never
happen again. I will also promise that
you will get alot of respect from now
on. Can you forgive me?

Love.
Adrian.

Adrian, age 9

Drawing yourself with an
exaggerated Italian mustache
renders the rest of your letter
insincere.

F

You are the greatest reading teacher. You make days great like Im riding on the back of a dragon. wich is very fun.

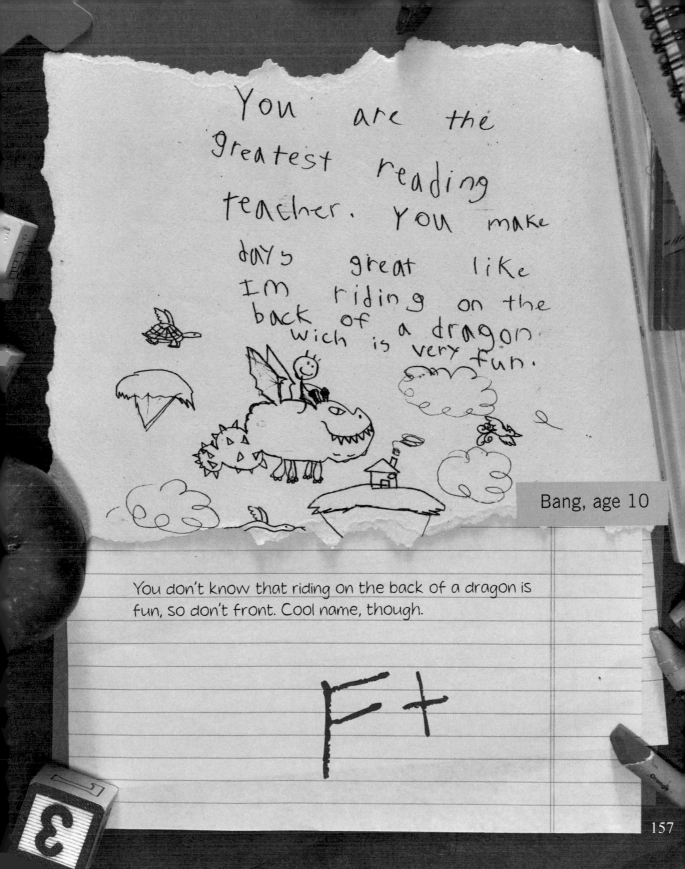

Bang, age 10

You don't know that riding on the back of a dragon is fun, so don't front. Cool name, though.

F+

Pictures

of

Kids

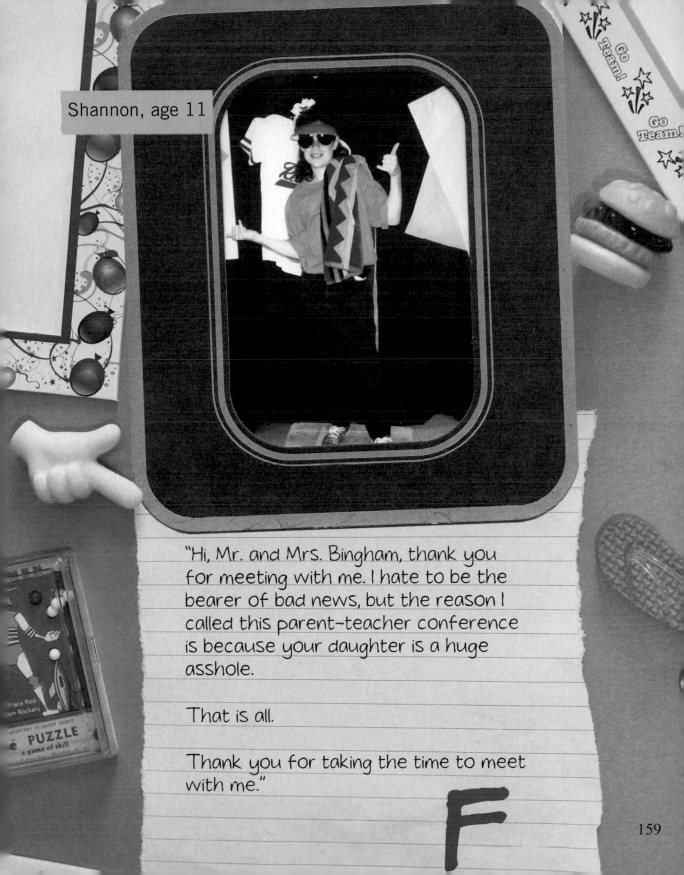

Shannon, age 11

"Hi, Mr. and Mrs. Bingham, thank you for meeting with me. I hate to be the bearer of bad news, but the reason I called this parent-teacher conference is because your daughter is a huge asshole.

That is all.

Thank you for taking the time to meet with me."

F

159

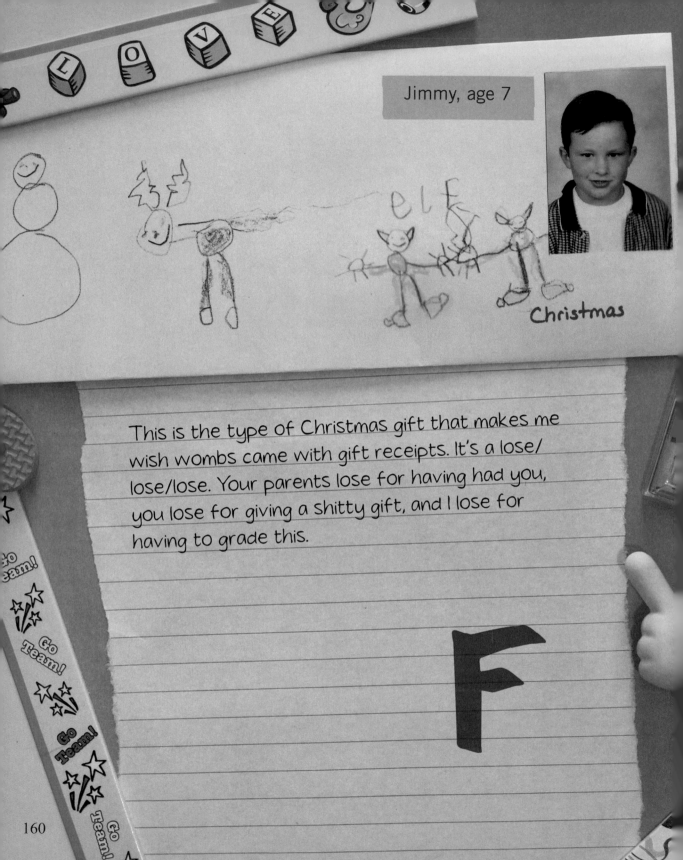

Jimmy, age 7

ELF

Christmas

This is the type of Christmas gift that makes me wish wombs came with gift receipts. It's a lose/lose/lose. Your parents lose for having had you, you lose for giving a shitty gift, and I lose for having to grade this.

F

Pedro, age 8

This is awesome.

F+

Batman: The Raped Crusader

Kids love Batman. I don't know why, because there are lots of superheroes and I don't think Batman is appreciably cooler than any other, except Superman, who's the dumbest fucking thing ever, but other than that, nothing. My working theory is that a lot of these kids made these around the time the last Batman movie came out. Whatever the reason, here are some of the best Batman submissions I received:

Is "Buttman" anything like Batman? Idiot.

My hero is Buttman

Billy, age 7

Batman is not a ninja turtle. And your name probably isn't Dude.

Dude, age 7

163

crate a new toy

If I crated a new toy ti would be a. Video game the them will be like Bat Man $ Call of duty. calld Call of Bat. You caoyd creat yor own caretor the rear can by Bat Man caretor's hear. The clows will de Call of duty pewter. The pack growh will be Call of Duty.

It will be rated E = 10 - M. It will be avaiblon DS $ Wii. It will be relly fun to play the game I might crat. So may be just may be, I could creat the game.

Call of Duty is one of the most successful franchises in video-game history, and Batman is one of the most successful franchises in comic books. And yet putting them together seems like a terrible idea. But put them together you did, Jacob. And what do you get? "Call of Bat," apparently. Not "Call of Duty: New Gotham," or even "Batman: Duty Calls," but "Call of Bat." Good attention to detail by rating it with the scientific notation E^{10}-M.

F ←

My hero is Bat Man.

BAT MAN

F

Jasmine, age 7

The *man* part of Batman is important, and this looks like a girl. If they had a female Batman, they'd call her something else. Oh yeah, they do: Bat Woman. Other egregious errors: she has whiskers like a cat, bird wings, and her name is written partly on her armpit.

Suraj, age 16

F

In this deleted scene from the blockbuster *The Dark Knight,* Batman savors a wistful moment before proceeding to give Joker a deep shoulder massage. Director Christopher Nolan opted to use an alternate facemask with askew eyebrows, concave right temple and beak-like nose for Batman and a cartoonishly small left hand for Joker.

167

Ages 1-6:
The Formative Years

Jared, age 3

Is it rude that I think this child has no future? I hope so!

F—

Kyley, age 1

Not only did someone take the time to date these scribbles, but they kept them around for over a quarter of a century. Crappy children's artwork is not like wine; it's not going to improve with age.

F—

11/9/85

Chan, age 5

pog

Wrong.

F

Doug, age 6

Bold choice to not have windows on your cop car. What are you policing? The Sun?

F

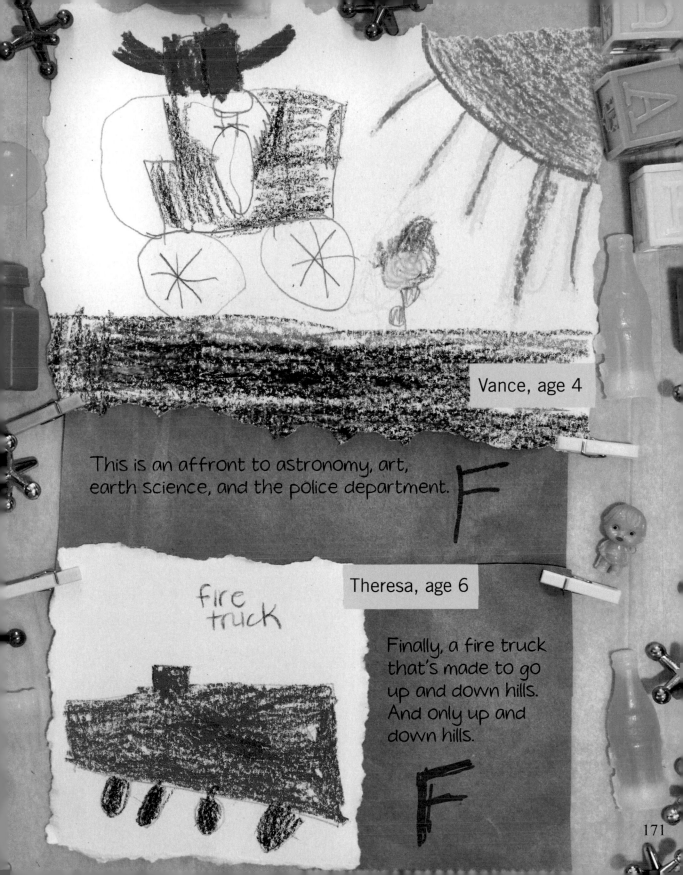

Vance, age 4

This is an affront to astronomy, art, earth science, and the police department. F

Theresa, age 6

fire truck

Finally, a fire truck that's made to go up and down hills. And only up and down hills.

F

When you spell "know" incorrectly in a sentence that begins with "I know a lot," it undermines your statement.

F

Emily, age 6

I No alot cat. likes to slep.

Nice tits.

F+

Chloe, age 5

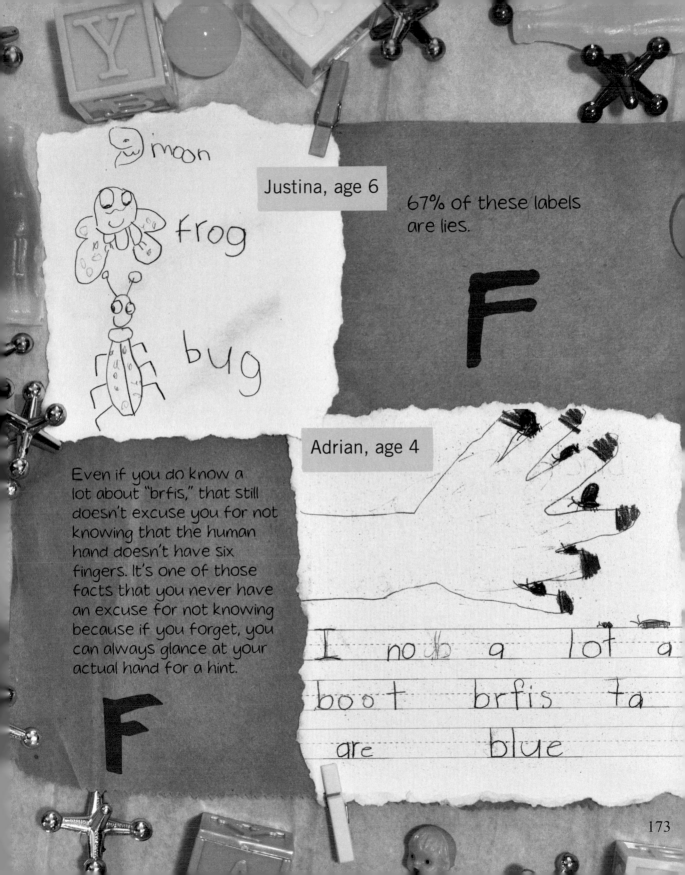

moon

frog

bug

67% of these labels are lies.

F

Even if you do know a lot about "brfis," that still doesn't excuse you for not knowing that the human hand doesn't have six fingers. It's one of those facts that you never have an excuse for not knowing because if you forget, you can always glance at your actual hand for a hint.

F

I no b a lot a
boot brfis ta
are blue

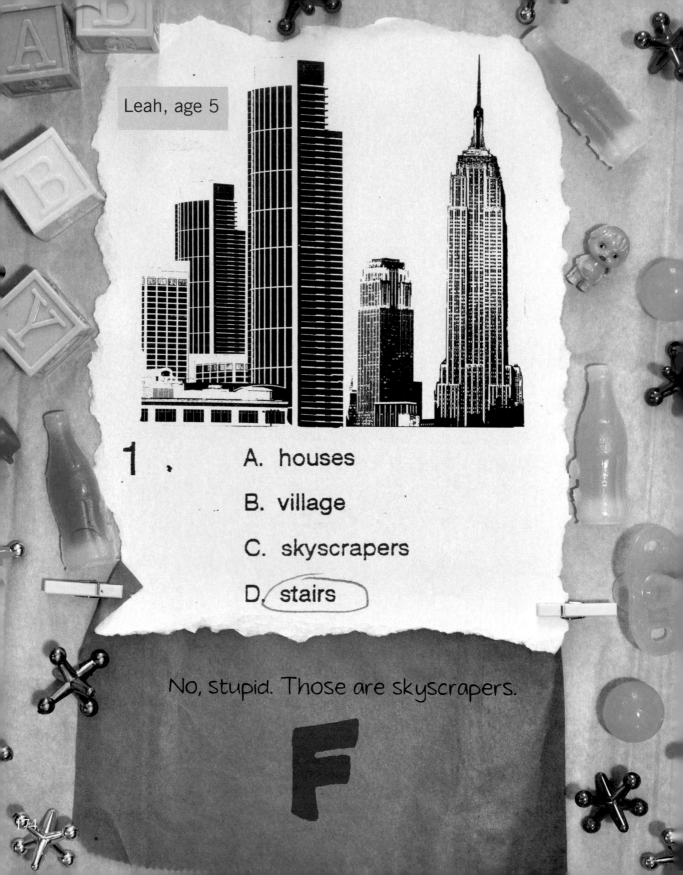

Leah, age 5

1. A. houses

   B. village

   C. skyscrapers

   D. stairs

No, stupid. Those are skyscrapers.

F

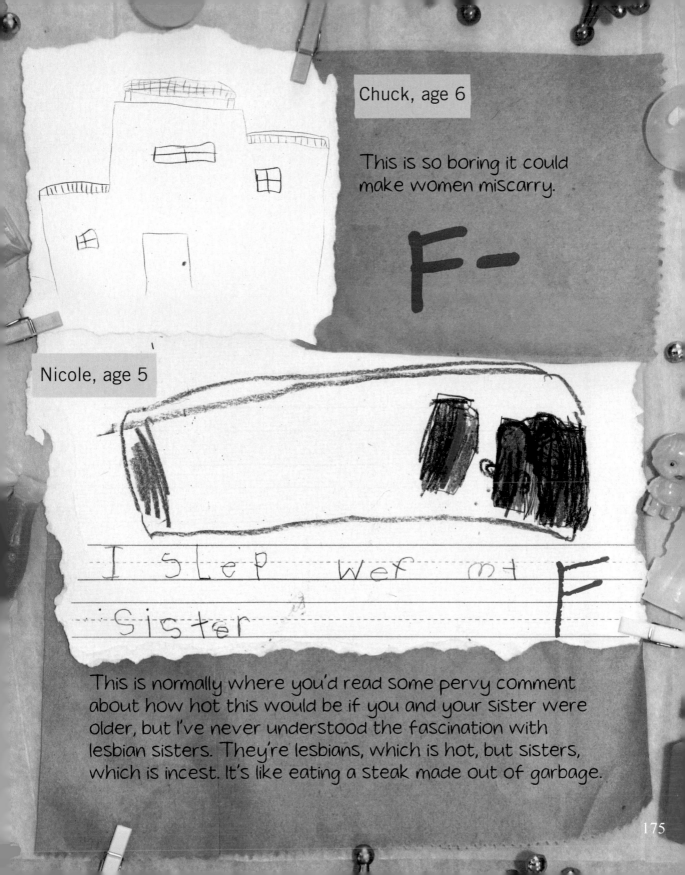

Chuck, age 6

This is so boring it could make women miscarry.

F-

Nicole, age 5

I sLeP weF mY sister

F

This is normally where you'd read some pervy comment about how hot this would be if you and your sister were older, but I've never understood the fascination with lesbian sisters. They're lesbians, which is hot, but sisters, which is incest. It's like eating a steak made out of garbage.

175

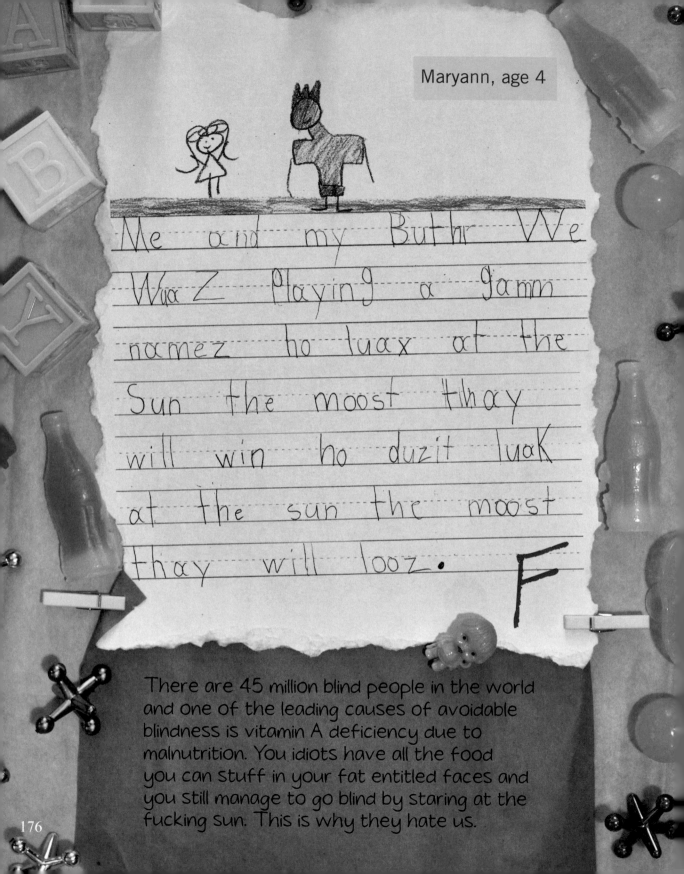

Maryann, age 4

Me and my Buthr We
Waz playing a gamm
namez ho tuax at the
Sun the moost thay
will win ho duzit luak
at the sun the moost
thay will looz. **F**

There are 45 million blind people in the world
and one of the leading causes of avoidable
blindness is vitamin A deficiency due to
malnutrition. You idiots have all the food
you can stuff in your fat entitled faces and
you still manage to go blind by staring at the
fucking sun. This is why they hate us.

Mary, age 6

Mr. Snuffles

bar

What is this? A cat or a dog? Trick question: it's kindling.

F

177

Meigha, age 4

I got hiv sore

I've never seen anyone who had HIV sores, and if this drawing is any indication, it's absolutely terrifying.

F

Joshua, age 1

This sucks the biggest donkey dick in the known universe, and some in multiverses we have yet to discover.

F−

Suzi, age 6

The assignment was to draw a coin. You traced a coin and drew a winking spoon.

F

Julie, age 5

It doesn't take a paleontologist to conclude that this dinosaur's diet consisted mostly of dicks.

F

insectosayrus

Nathan, age 6

This is either really bad, or really modern.

F

POPSICLE STICK

"Hi, I'm a giant joint. Bet you weren't expecting to find me in a kindergartner's drawing, and yet, here I am."

F

Kami, age 6

SHELB
SHELBY
F

This was sent to me by Shelby's father asking for my opinion as a professional art critic, as I am most certainly that. Shelby and her mother disagree with her father's assertion that cats don't have chicken legs. This has not, and will never be up for debate because anything after the word "chicken" in the sentence "a cat has chicken . . ." is false. Shelby's father has won the battle, but lost the war, because his wife and daughter are imbeciles.

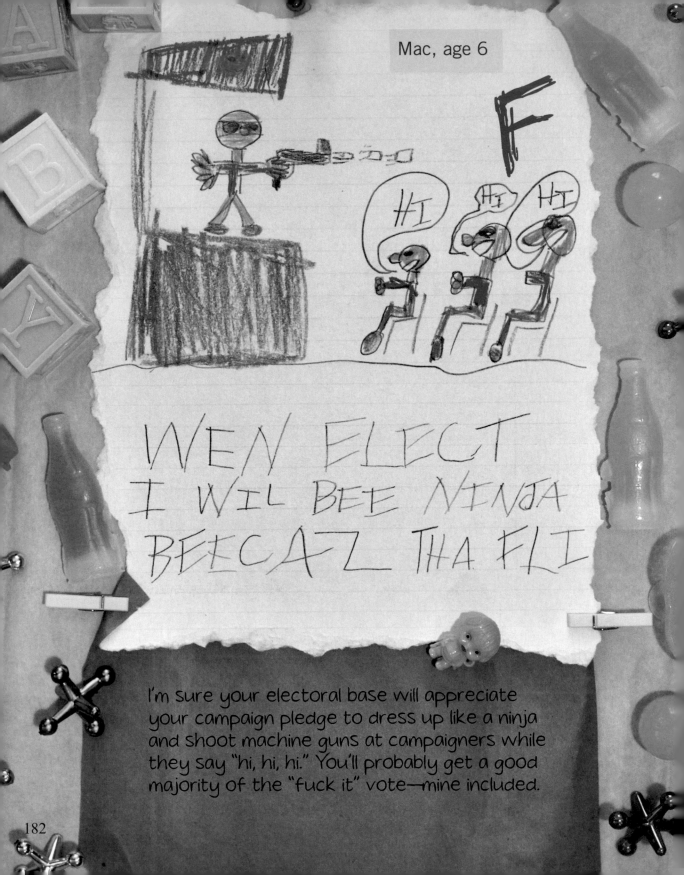

I'm sure your electoral base will appreciate your campaign pledge to dress up like a ninja and shoot machine guns at campaigners while they say "hi, hi, hi." You'll probably get a good majority of the "fuck it" vote—mine included.

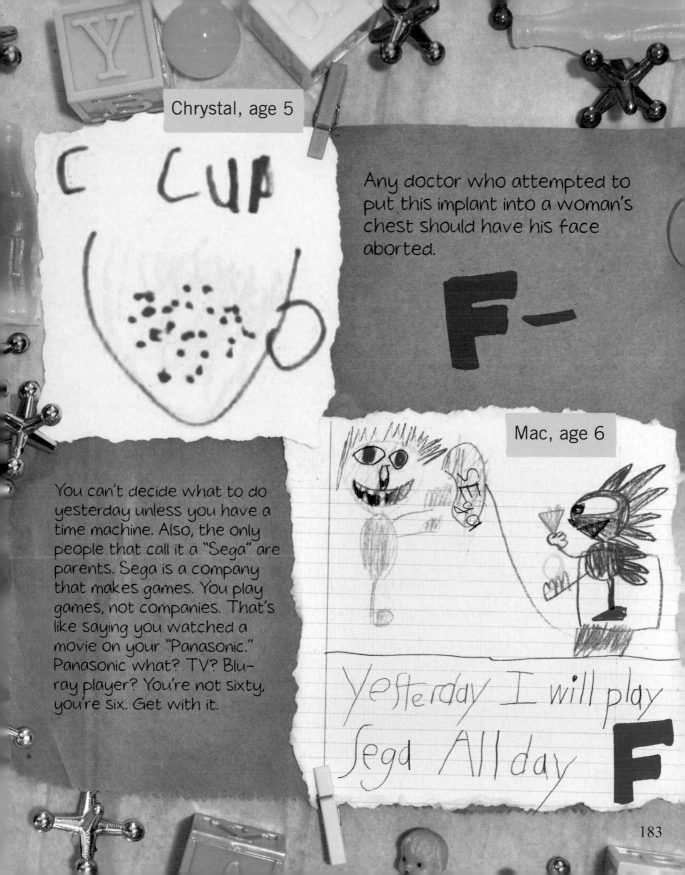

Chrystal, age 5

C CUP

Any doctor who attempted to put this implant into a woman's chest should have his face aborted.

F-

Mac, age 6

You can't decide what to do yesterday unless you have a time machine. Also, the only people that call it a "Sega" are parents. Sega is a company that makes games. You play games, not companies. That's like saying you watched a movie on your "Panasonic." Panasonic what? TV? Blu-ray player? You're not sixty, you're six. Get with it.

Yesterday I will play Sega All day

F

Ne and ben going to the soo too shicrshit.

F

Randy, age 6

If you want a child to get over his speech impediment quickly, don't correct him when he says "shic-r-shit" while trick-or-treating on Halloween. Nothing fixes lazy enunciation faster than asking for candy and getting a sack of shit instead.

You have managed to take crappy drawings to the third dimension. That is, you are using the requisite red and blue colors for 3-D, but when nothing is lost or gained with 3-D glasses, it means you're missing the point. You have a very promising career in Hollywood ahead of you.

F

Chuck, age 5

A carrot climbed on a bay.

F

How about a little humility? Not everything you write needs to be read by others.

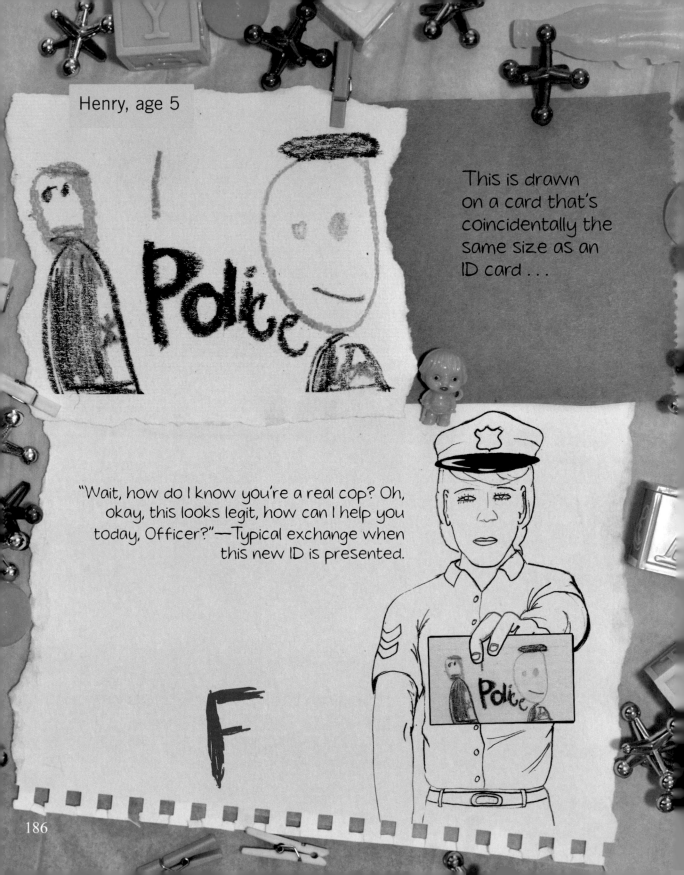

Henry, age 5

This is drawn on a card that's coincidentally the same size as an ID card . . .

"Wait, how do I know you're a real cop? Oh, okay, this looks legit, how can I help you today, Officer?"—Typical exchange when this new ID is presented.

Joel, age 6

sKAry And
Viprs

What is that? A castle?
A stapler? Well, anyway,
you failed kindergarten.

F

Fiona, age 6

This is just as much a
constable's hat as it is a
vehicle.

F

A Mouse climbed on a house.

Natalie, age 5

AND? Then what? You think you're so special that you can just spit out any little turd your untalented fingers can scrawl and people will just eat it up? Get bent.

F-

I See A bro and a Rambo This Da wus Fun

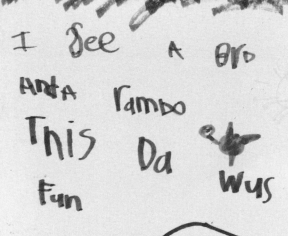

First of all, there is only one Rambo, so saying you saw "a" Rambo implies there are others. And second, there is no second. How does it feel to be misled?

F

Kyley, age 4

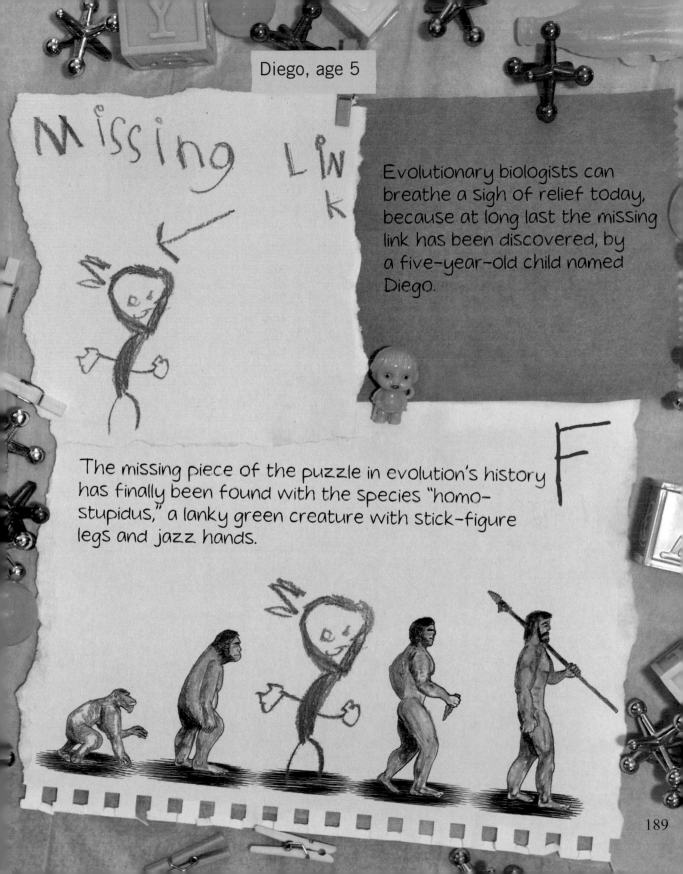

Diego, age 5

Missing Link

Evolutionary biologists can breathe a sigh of relief today, because at long last the missing link has been discovered, by a five-year-old child named Diego.

The missing piece of the puzzle in evolution's history has finally been found with the species "homo-stupidus," a lanky green creature with stick-figure legs and jazz hands.

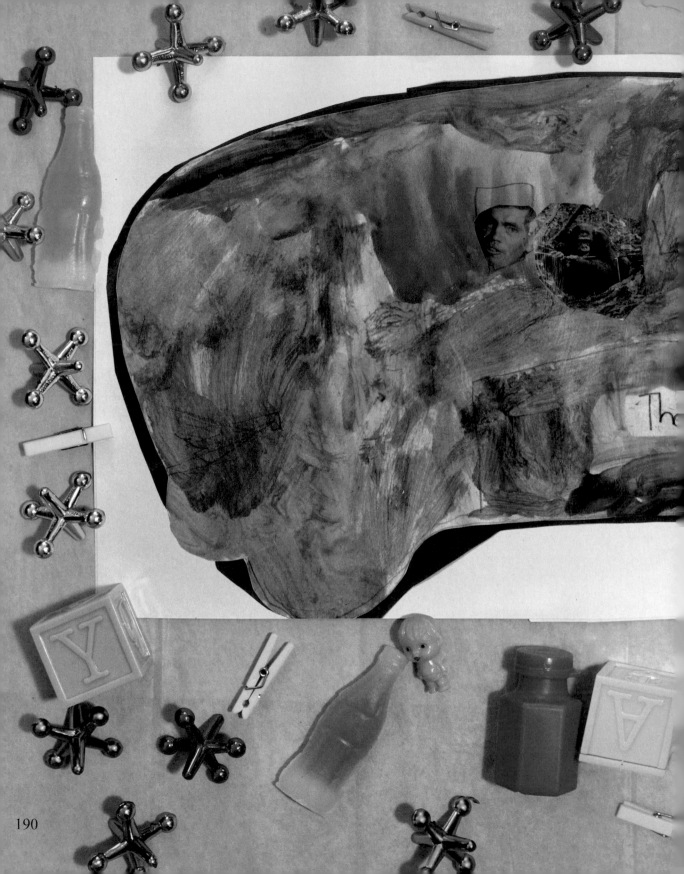

190

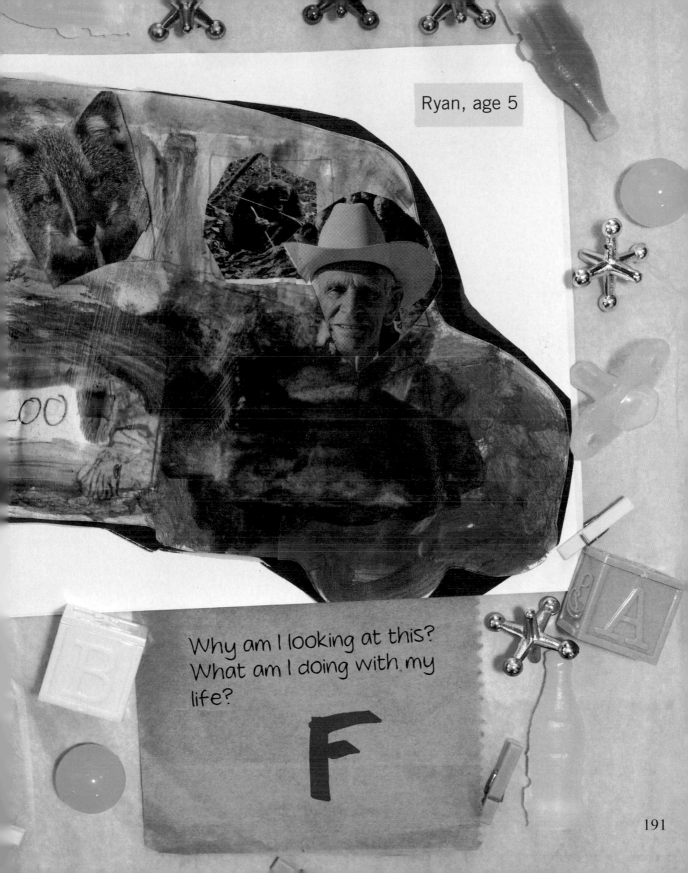

Ryan, age 5

Why am I looking at this?
What am I doing with my
life?

F

Geoff, age 6

The Three Bears

"Someone's been sleeping in my bed!" said Papa Bear.
Someone's been sleeping in my bed too!" said Mama Bear.
"..." said NINJA BEAR.

Just then, Goldilocks woke up to find her THROAT
CHOPPED OPEN AND HER SEVERED HEAD LOOKING
DOWN AT THE REST OF HER BODY FROM ATOP THE
BEDPOST. Ninja bear stands with his back turned to
her. He sheaths his sword, sits down cross-legged, and
levitates like it ain't no thang.

F+

Ages 7–14:
The Aftermath

Pokie Little Puppie

This is Poky Little Puppy from the eponymous children's book. At first glance, I suspected this was traced, so I held the paper up to the light . . .

Eloisee, age 7

F . . . and sure enough, it's tracing paper. It bears only a passing resemblance to the original book cover, which suggests it's hand drawn, but if that's the case, why the tracing paper? That's like bringing a gun to a knife fight and throwing the gun at your assailant.

The Little Mermade

This sketch is 36 by 26.5 inches. That's 954 square inches of pure crap!

F

Jamie, age 7

I guess sometimes ninjas poop in bowls.

F+

Richard, age 13

Friedrich, age 10

Jesus was not burned at the stake as a witch.

F

Karl, age 9

The knees
are totally
unprotected.

F

196

Michael, age 9

What are the four main Native American environments?
1. Pacific Ocean
2. Indiana Ocean
3. Artic Ocean
4. Altlantic Ocean
} What??

What continent do you live in? ~~South America~~
What country do you live in? ~~California~~
What state do you live in? ~~Los Angeles~~

Michael,
I'm disappointed :-(

Michael, unlike your teacher, you did not disappoint me. I had no expectations for you, and you met my expectations.

F

Tom, age 12

That's one sad, fat dragon. Villagers go straight to her thighs.

F

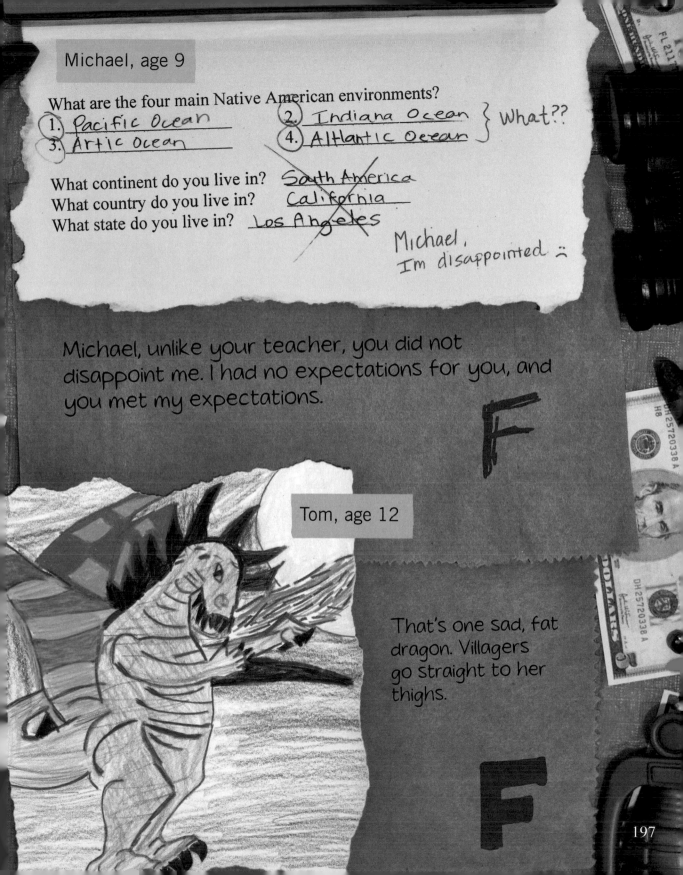

Margeaux, age 8

Minou

This cat is bending space-time around it like a black hole. Even the bird is getting sucked in while desperately trying to fly away. Why aren't all drawings of cats like this?

F+

Kyle, age 12

No matter who wins, some future employer will lose.

F

DRACULA VS. KYLE

198

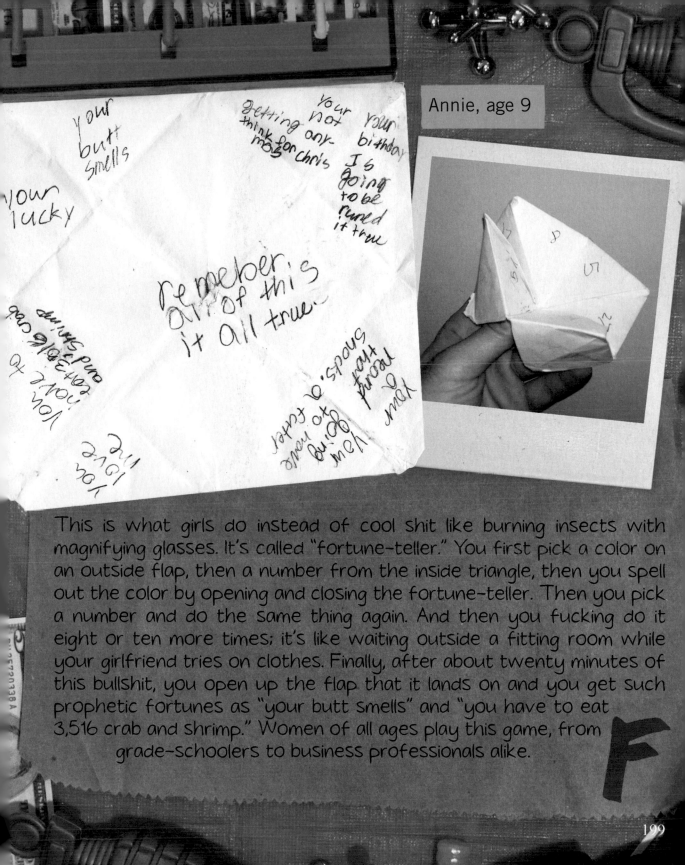

your butt smells

your lucky

getting any think for Chris mas

your not birthday is going to be ruined it true

remeber all of this it all true

you have to eat 3,516 crab and shrimp

you love lil

you're going to have a sore throat

Annie, age 9

This is what girls do instead of cool shit like burning insects with magnifying glasses. It's called "fortune-teller." You first pick a color on an outside flap, then a number from the inside triangle, then you spell out the color by opening and closing the fortune-teller. Then you pick a number and do the same thing again. And then you fucking do it eight or ten more times; it's like waiting outside a fitting room while your girlfriend tries on clothes. Finally, after about twenty minutes of this bullshit, you open up the flap that it lands on and you get such prophetic fortunes as "your butt smells" and "you have to eat 3,516 crab and shrimp." Women of all ages play this game, from grade-schoolers to business professionals alike.

F

Jon, age 8

F

Boop boop WoooOOOooo! "Officer shit-cop here, how may I assist?" You can start by shaving your junk heap of a cruiser and removing two of the wheels so it's no longer a Zamboni.

Byron, age 13

I suppose there were transvestites in the Middle Ages, and transvestite dragons probably kidnapped them on occasion. I never thought I'd have to entertain the concept of a dragon with a man-pussy. I miss two minutes ago. Those were more innocent times.

F

200

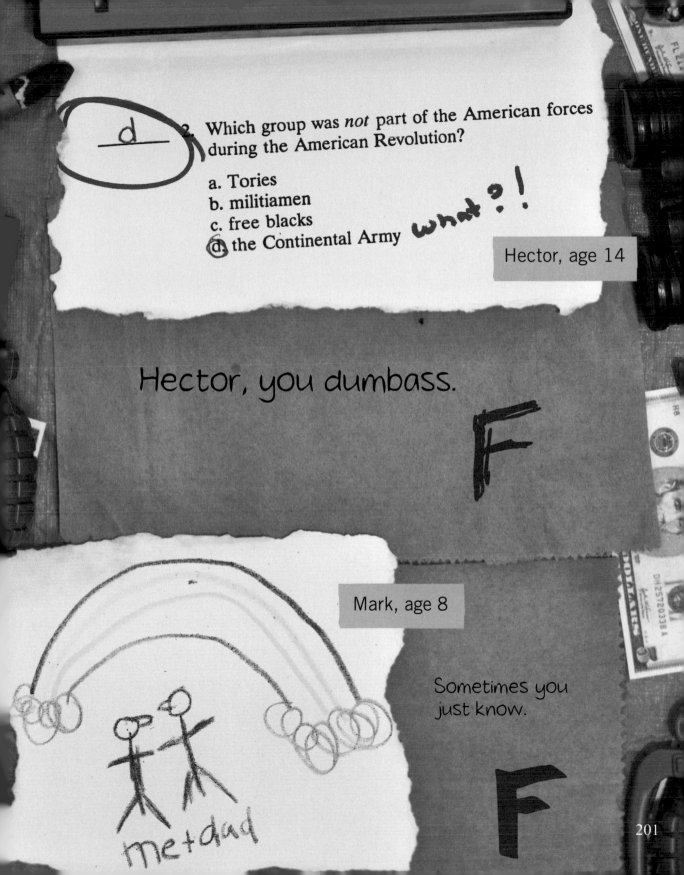

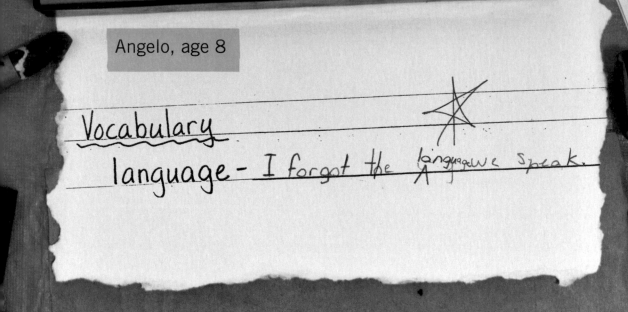

Angelo, age 8

Vocabulary

language - I forgot the ~~language~~ A speak.

This paradox threatens to implode
our universe.

F

Erik, age 14

This 2.5-dimensional
gun has a
2-dimensional stock
that gives stick
figures easy gripping,
but a 3-dimensional
barrel that can kill
actual people.

F+

Andre, age 7

"Hello, my friend! I have number one game for you! Please step into my alley, I have Sonic the Hedj Hug, he is fast guy with beer belly. I give you good price!"

Sonic The Hedj Hug

Tabatha, age 10

write more please

Comphrehension

I'm actually going to disagree with your teacher: write less. Like 100% less.

Andre, age 7

Good job on the selective coloring;
looks just like a screen shot:

204

Goldilocks and the 3 hunks (the modern version)

Once there was a girl called Goldilocks, She loved rings, Heck! She had nose rings, bellybutton rings, and earrings. (5 holes in each ear.) well, anyways, she was always trying to get into mischief. So one day she snuck into an old abandoned house. She was surprised to see that there were three hunks staring at her. "wow!" she thought. "what hunks!" The first hunk said, "your too SMALL!" The 2nd hunk said, "your too FAT!!" But! The 3rd hunk said. "Heh, heh, heh! You're just right." So now Goldie girl lives in a huge mansion off the coast of Puerto Rico with a buff hunk who's name is 3rd choice.

Marrying someone whose name is "3rd choice" is so real it gives fat waitresses in truck-stop diners everywhere a run for their money.

F+

We are the world

Me haha ha

Black people have faces and Asian people's eyes don't actually slant.

F

205

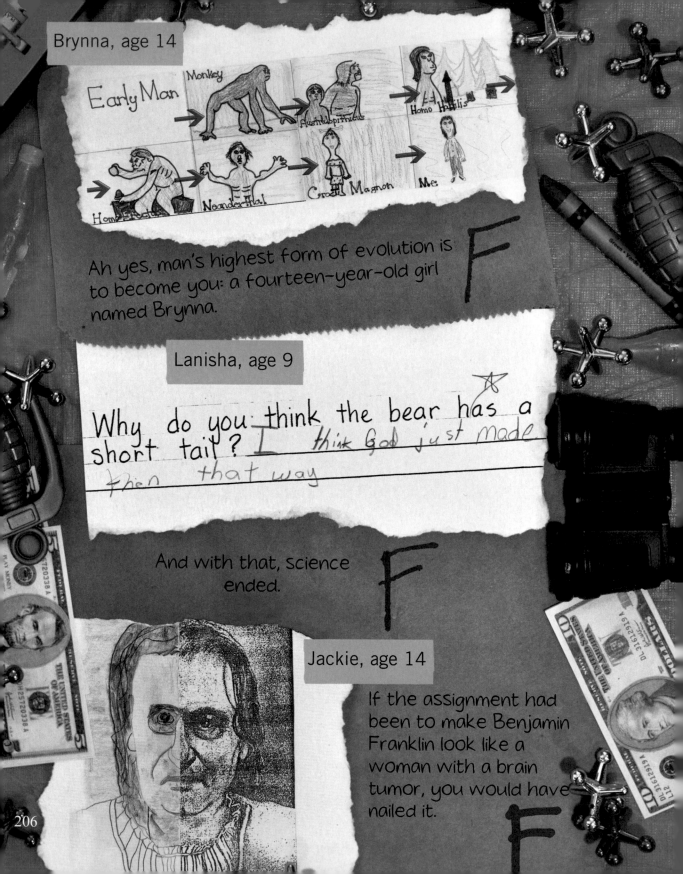

Brynna, age 14

Early Man   Monkey   Australopithecus   Homo Habilis

Homo Erectus   Neanderthal   Cro Magnon   Me

Ah yes, man's highest form of evolution is to become you: a fourteen-year-old girl named Brynna.

F

Lanisha, age 9

Why do you think the bear has a short tail? I think God just made him that way

And with that, science ended.

F

Jackie, age 14

If the assignment had been to make Benjamin Franklin look like a woman with a brain tumor, you would have nailed it.

F

Make a list:

Timothy, age 10

Things glasses <u>can</u> improve	Things glasses <u>can not</u> improve
reading writing cutting glueing	Playing Cluminess Singing

Clumsiness cannot be improved with glasses; however, the spelling of "cluminess" can.

F

Jake, age 8

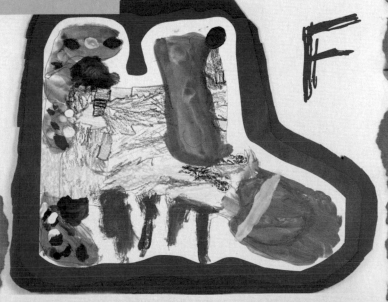

F

I was at a party in New York a few years ago when I got so drunk that I threw up all over my shoes. Even puke-covered, my shoes still looked better than this. I've literally barfed more coherently than this child's art. That makes me a winner.

Seal Looking at Scribbles

Nathan, age 9

Marker on paper

This monk seal is looking wistfully at a jumble of scribbles off in the distance, or possibly right in front of him; it's hard to tell due to the young artist's avoidance of depth and shading. Note the orange carelessly floating behind the seal for no fucking reason.

Carolann, age 11

8:51 P.M
AUGUST
17th,
1996

"Excuse me, ma'am. When did your daughter create this drawing?"

"August seventeenth, 1996. Why, is something wrong, Officer?"

"What time?"

"I believe it was 8:51 P.M."

"No problem, just checking to make sure your child's artwork had the proper documentation. Carry on."

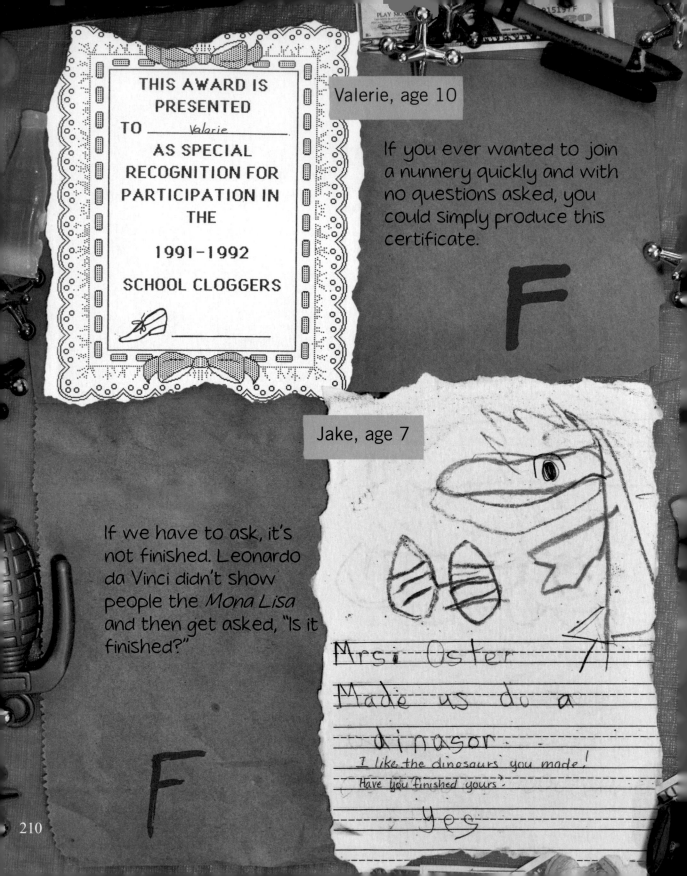

THIS AWARD IS PRESENTED

TO _Valerie_

AS SPECIAL RECOGNITION FOR PARTICIPATION IN THE

1991–1992

SCHOOL CLOGGERS

Valerie, age 10

If you ever wanted to join a nunnery quickly and with no questions asked, you could simply produce this certificate.

F

Jake, age 7

If we have to ask, it's not finished. Leonardo da Vinci didn't show people the *Mona Lisa* and then get asked, "Is it finished?"

F

Mrs. Oster
Made us do a
dinasor
I like the dinosaurs you made!
Have you finished yours?
Yes

210

THE DIGESTIVE SYSTEM

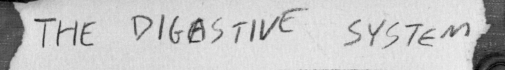

Noel, age 10

MOUTH

ESOPHIGUS
(FOOD TUBE)

STOMACH

SMALL INTESTINE

BIG INTESTINE

BUTTHOLE

That's not a medical term. If you ever hear a so-called doctor say, "Now turn around and let me take a look at your butthole," run.

F

211

Wish

What are some things that you regret doing?

(1) I wish I had studied harder for my math test.
(2) I wish I hadn't wore my dirty pants today.

Don't just sit there wishing for a change of pants. Be the change of pants you want to see in the world. Yeah, bitch, you just got dissed Gandhi-style.

F

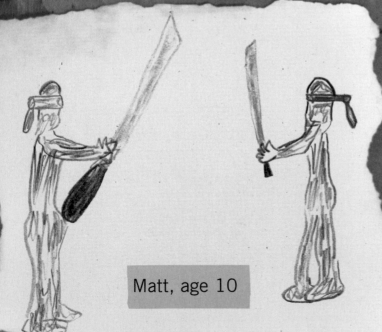

Matt, age 10

If you draw a couple of dudes literally sword fighting, they already look like they're metaphorically sword fighting. You don't need to gild the lily with actual boners.

F

CRIME AND PUNISHMENT

What happens if . . .

. . . you don't do your homework?

_____ you die _____

Aurthur, age 11

Yes, correct. You die. **F+**

What I like about this worksheet is that you clearly don't give a fuck, and yet you erased your answer to the question "What is the longest river in Africa?" and changed it to "cups."

Fastest, Longest, Biggest

Brandt, age 11

What is the biggest mountain in the world?

pudding

What is the biggest mountain in Japan?

cookies

What is the fastest animal in the world?

lions

What is the biggest animal in the world?

dragon

What is the biggest country in the world?

USA

What is the richest country in the world?

F+

What is the longest river in Africa?

cups

What is the longest river in South America?

Denny, age 11

If I Were A.... ? Worksheet
Animals

1. Choose an animal you would like to be. Pretend you are this animal for the remaining questions.	*cat*
	Animals Name
	~~dog,~~ people, zombies,
2. Describe your natural enemies.	

F−

Way to go all out on the creativity scale by picking a cat. And for the record, the number of cats that die every year from zombie outbreaks is zero.

Dictionary Skills

Jason, age 10

Directions: Using a dictionary, find the answer to each of the following scenarios.

1. If you were **beautifying** your neighborhood park, what might you be doing to it?

making it look spectacular

2. If you didn't understand the **lingo** used in a book, what don't you understand?

what it ment

3. If an artist asked to hold their **palette**, what would you be holding?

proboblay thure micoophone

"Proboblay there microphone" is not the answer to any question.

F

Wesley, age 8

Drag queen of the jungle?

F

214

Stone, age 12

What animals are at the top of the food chain?

Beer, egl, Deer,
Bee, Grass, Flower

Every scientist knows that the food chain starts with malted-barley beverages, eagles, deer, and bees, and ends with predators like grass and flowers.

F

the mexican war staltes
1846

Pat, age 9

The Mexican-American War was indeed a time of great strife for the Super Mario Brothers.

F

I would . . .

What would you do if you had 1 million dollars?
buy a pool of pudding with a submarine

What would you do if you saw a bear in the forest?
ask a scientist

F

A submarine in a pool of pudding? That's like a fat kid's dream. Way to blow a million dollars, fatty.

And where would you find a scientist in the forest? They wouldn't just be hanging around, waiting for random sixth-graders to ask them questions about bears. Scientists have shit to do.

Tim, age 11

Relax, Tim, worksheets that ask you to "pretend" shouldn't stress you out this much.

If I Were A.... ? Worksheet

Animals

1. Choose an animal you would like to be. Pretend you are this animal for the remaining questions.	<u>Animal</u> **Animals Name**
2. Describe your natural enemies.	<u>Pizza, veggies, donuts, etc.</u>
3. What do you eat?	<u>Wood.</u>
4. Where do you live?	<u>Candy land.</u>
5. Do humans help or hurt you? Why?	I DON'T KNOW

China: Stereotypes and Prejudices Worksheet

1. What stereotypes do North Americans have of people of the Chinese culture?

   That they have slanted eyes.

2. Why do you feel people hold these stereotypes?

   Because they have slanted eyes.

3. Why is it extremely important to not stereotype, or profile any given culture?

   Because it is mean, cruel, rude, and unproffesional.

You are failing to connect the dots here.

Questions On The Civil War

1. Who was the president of the United States during the Civil War?

   Harry Potter

2. Who was the vice president of the United States during the Civil War?

   Me~

3. Who was the president of the Confederate States?

   King Spagetti

   Kevo, age 12

4. Who was the commander of the army of the Confederate States?

   Darth Vader.

You're not even trying.

F-

Ralph, age 8

B is for Bovine

No, B is for Boners.
Read up on your
classic literature.

F

This is how I look when I feel **angry**:

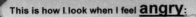

This is both creepy and super cool.

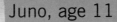

F+

I feel angry when:

I sleep

This is how I look when I feel **angry**:

This is the exact same face I make when I'm hunting for treasure in caverns with my friends Chunk, Mouth and Data.

F

I feel angry when: When I don't get what I want.

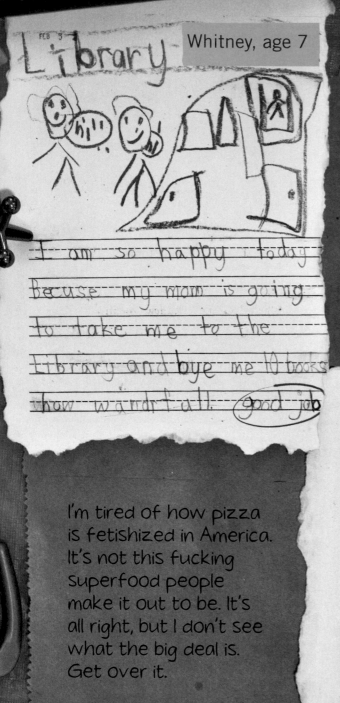

Library

FEB 5

I am so happy today Becuse my mom is going to take me to the Library and bye me 10 books how wandr ful. good job

I'm a big fan of congratulating myself when nobody else does it for me. Good job (that was to me).

F

I'm tired of how pizza is fetishized in America. It's not this fucking superfood people make it out to be. It's all right, but I don't see what the big deal is. Get over it.

F−

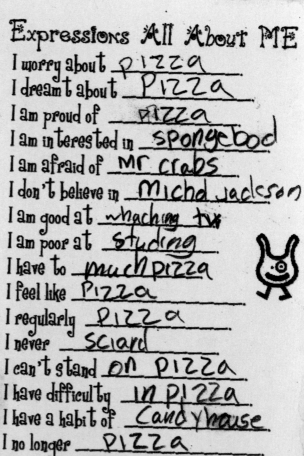

Expressions All About ME

I worry about ___ pizza
I dreamt about ___ pizza
I am proud of ___ pizza
I am interested in ___ spongebod
I am afraid of ___ Mr crabs
I don't believe in ___ Michd jacleson
I am good at ___ whaching tvs
I am poor at ___ studing
I have to ___ much pizza
I feel like ___ pizza
I regularly ___ pizza
I never ___ sciard
I can't stand ___ on pizza
I have difficulty ___ in pizza
I have a habit of ___ Candyhouse
I no longer ___ pizza

This should just read "Loser."

F

PARKS &
RECREATION
DEPARTMENT

FOURTH
PLACE

Simon, age 8

Shark bite Fite!

Booker, age 9

That's how I'd dispatch a shark, too.

F+

221

What You Want to Be
When You Grow Up

ZOMBE

RIP

Kim, age 10

You want to grow up to be a mindless zombie? This actually seems likely. BOOM.

F

Garo, age 6

This is the saddest-looking weight lifter I've ever seen. He looks like two hundred pounds of munged assholes. This droopy look is enough to make chicks go into menopause.

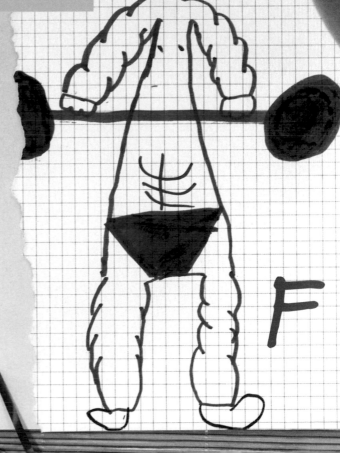

F

223

What a coincidence: you want to grow up to be posessed by a poltergeist in a haunted house, and I want to become an evil spirit who haunts children after I die. Let's talk.

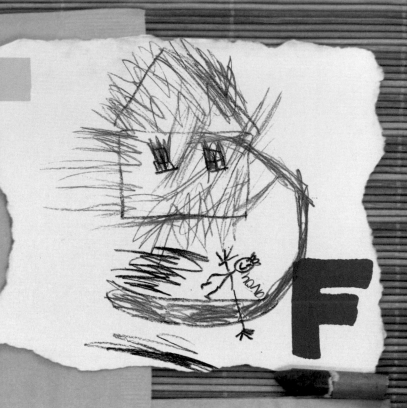

Jacqueline, age 4

I have some good news and bad news, Jacqueline:

The bad news is that you can't become a teacher because you can't spell.

The good news is that McDonald's can look forward to hiring you when you're sixteen. But only for nine months, until you go into labor.

Seks

F

- Polismen forer

You want to have sex with policemen forever? That's a disturbing commitment.

Upon glancing, one might think little Jade is making an admirable career choice to be a teacher . . . until you notice that there's a MOTHERFUCKING BED IN THE CLASSROOM! Red flag!

Teacher

Abed

F

Jade, age 5

Molly, age 5

Good news, Molly. Since
you're built like a pole,
you actually have a
really good shot at being
a "tether."

F

ncn I Grow uP I
vant to be a Teeh er
will love to be a
tether.

Fernando, age 6

With the right combination
of greasy food and
a lighter, anyone can
become a "firefarter."

F

Balderer

Dog

F

Bad news, Susan. You can't be much balder than this.

227

Creepy Clowns

Ken, age 10

Is there a norm that all clowns aspire to, or are they all just doomed to look like people who'd feel at home with your kidneys simmering on their stoves? Maybe I'm projecting. But still.

I've never been raped by a clown, but I suspect this is the last thing you'd see before it happened.

Cory, age 8

Alyssa, age 11

Rob & JD, age 10

This is what it would look like if you could paint with a palette made entirely of children's nightmares.

F

Here we go. You know this guy has seen problems something fierce. This motherfucker is the real deal.

F+

230

Your Dream Pet

Irving, age 5

I wyt a cat becaus is a eat

I can only infer that you want to eat your cat. Awesome.

F+

Dog

I would be sad too if I looked like a smashed asshole.

F

Genevieve, age 4

232

F

poler bear

Melaina, age 6

Life is not a cartoon where you and your trendy friends stand around with a FUCKING POLAR BEAR in the room. These animals are vicious killing machines.

This is what your encounter with the polar bear would really look like:

Maddox, age 32

A+

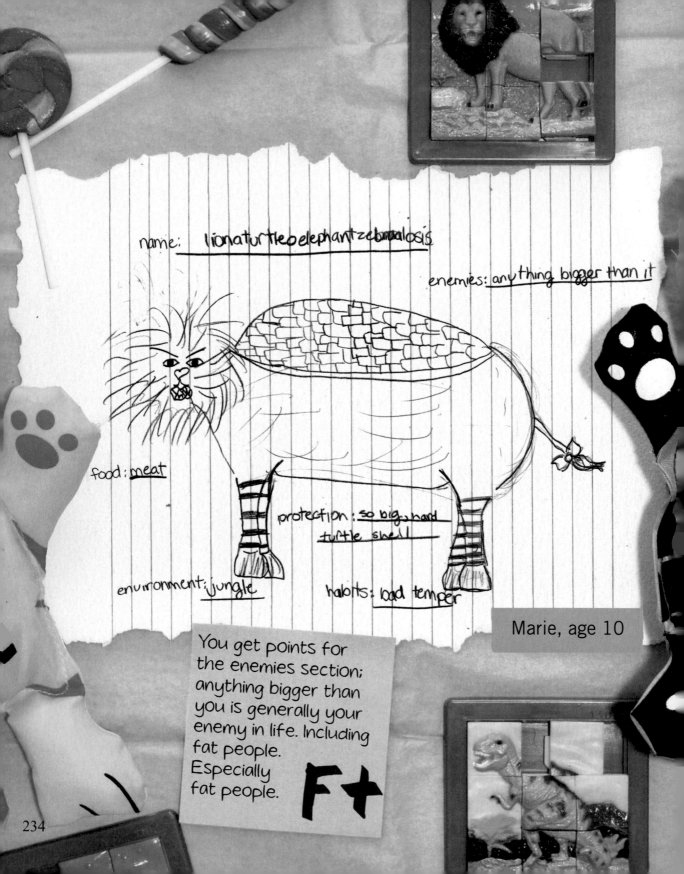

name: lionaturtleoelephantzebraalosis

enemies: anything bigger than it

food: meat

protection: so big, hard turtle shell

environment: jungle

habits: bad temper

Marie, age 10

You get points for the enemies section; anything bigger than you is generally your enemy in life. Including fat people. Especially fat people.

F+

234

Ralph, age 6

My goal in life is to witness enough astonishing shit to constantly look as surprised as everything in this drawing.

F+

Tiger

Your pet tiger is either horny or retarded. For the sake of decorum, I'm eliminating the possibility that he could be both.

F

Dax, age 6

235

3+3=d. 3+2=?

No, 3 + 3 ≠ d. Also, this has nothing to do with anything.

F =

Billy, age 6

236

Not Picasso

237

Arthur, age 8

It's said that art should make a statement. And I believe the statement this art is making is: "fuck it."

I have a sneaking suspicion that Pablo Picasso didn't make this.

Pablo Picasso?

1881
pablo
picasso

238

239

Alan, age 7

Finally a roller coaster for people who want to experience the thrill of death.

F

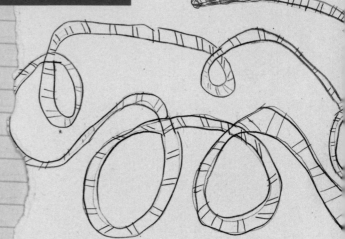

I can only assume that the person about to kill himself on the carousel is the park owner, because even he doesn't understand what the fuck happened to his roller coaster.

F

Arthur, age 7

A'darrion, age 7

Thank you for saving me the trouble of scribbling all over this.

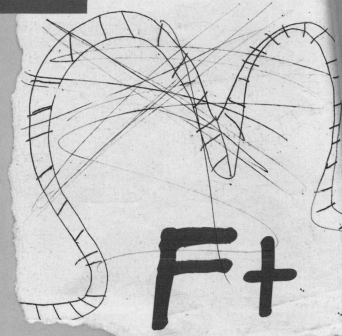

This sucks. You suck. Check out my roller coaster on the next page.

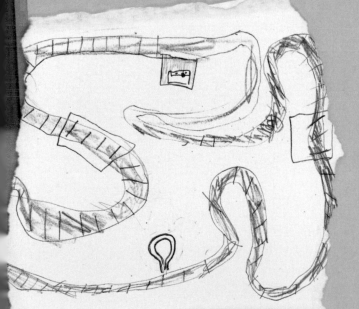

Justin, age 6

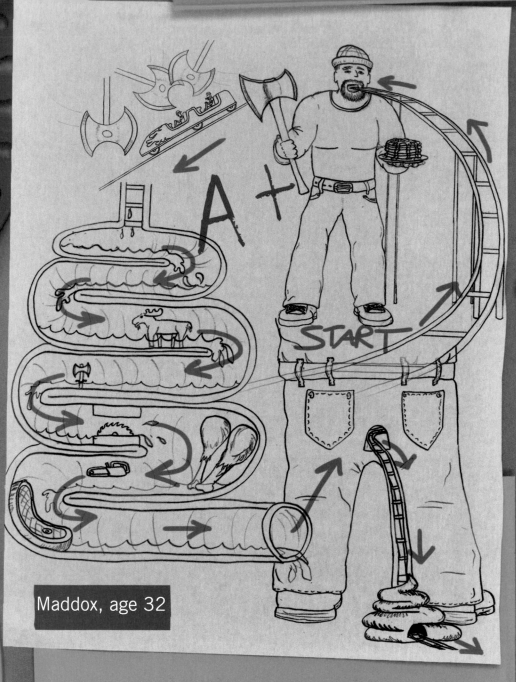

Maddox, age 32

BAM! This is so awesome it makes my balls ache. This coaster takes you through a lumberjack's bowels, out his pooper, and through a pile of lumberjack turds. Awesome and classy!

Queer for a Day

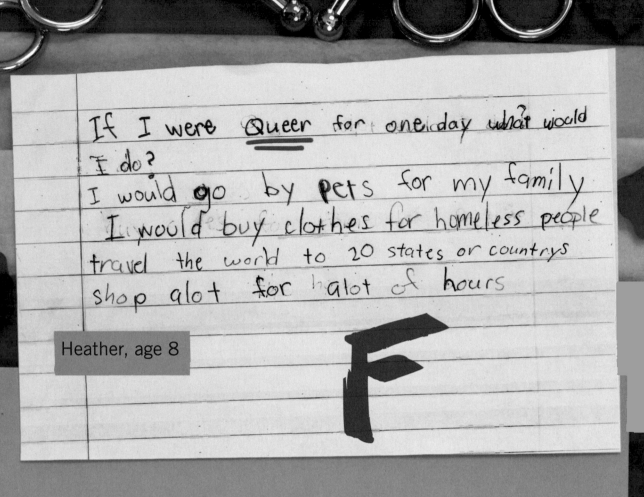

If I were <u>Queer</u> for one day what would I do?

I would go by pets for my family
I would buy clothes for homeless people
travel the world to 20 states or countrys
shop alot for a lot of hours

Heather, age 8

F

Did you mean to write "queen"? Because if I were queer for a day, I'd probably buy some denim capris and do some gay shit.

The Biggest Problem in the World Today

Many people believe that children have unique insights into the world and can see solutions to problems where none exist. So I asked kids what they thought the biggest problem in the world was today. Their answers were enlightening, not because they had a unique ability to observe problems we've taken for granted, but because their problems were incredibly myopic or self-serving: homework or earthquakes. Here's a small sample of the nonproblems chosen by children:

SHOoL

Tetsuo, age 8

When you want to make the case that there's too much school in the world today, spelling the word "school" correctly will bolster your case.

F

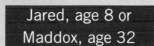

Jared, age 8 or
Maddox, age 32

School is The Biggest in The World

F

I had so many submissions about school being the biggest problem in the world today, that I started to believe it, renounced my education, and ate a box of crayons. My subsequent bowel movement was this drawing.

Buildings falling on teepee villages would indeed be a problem today if structural engineers suddenly became morons . . . and people still lived in teepee villages.

F

Brent, age 8

fallen building

Cracked floors

247

Can you imagine lawmakers on Capitol Hill debating what to do with gum wrappers? Me neither.

Joseph, age 9

There is so much wrong with this picture. First, how could there be no water in the North Pole? Even the most aggressive global-warming models don't predict total evaporation of the oceans. They do, however, predict a rise in ocean levels due to the melting of polar ice caps. Which leads me to the next problem: if the ice caps have melted, then how is the penguin still standing on ice? And if it's hot enough for oceans to evaporate, how is one solitary penguin still alive? And why are there penguins at the North Pole anyway? Penguins live in the South Pole. Also, if all the water evaporated on earth, people would be dying of dehydration and famine. WHO GIVES A SHIT ABOUT A SINGLE PENGUIN?

249

Mario, age 9

That's rather presumptuous.

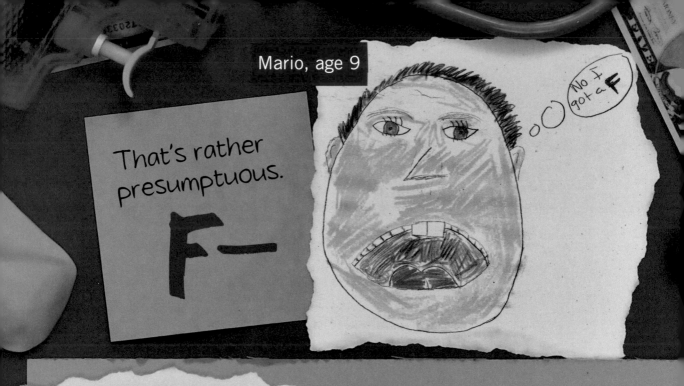

Rosa, age 9

Words like "before" and "after" are weasel words because they aren't being used to qualify anything. Before what? You should be ashamed of yourself.

Janice, age 9

Yeah, actually. Hippies are a huge problem today.

F+

Gail, age 9

Way to be a bitter man-hating crone at age nine. You're going to make some unlucky man very miserable someday.

F-

What is the biggest problem in the world... oh yeah... Boys.

Ellyn, age 9

Way to illustrate the devastation of an earthquake by drawing a bird's nest falling out of a tree. That really drove the point home.

F

If the monkeys escaped at the zoo, people wouldn't stand around yelling, "Zoo!" That would be like cops called to investigate a shooting and yelling, "Crime scene!"

F

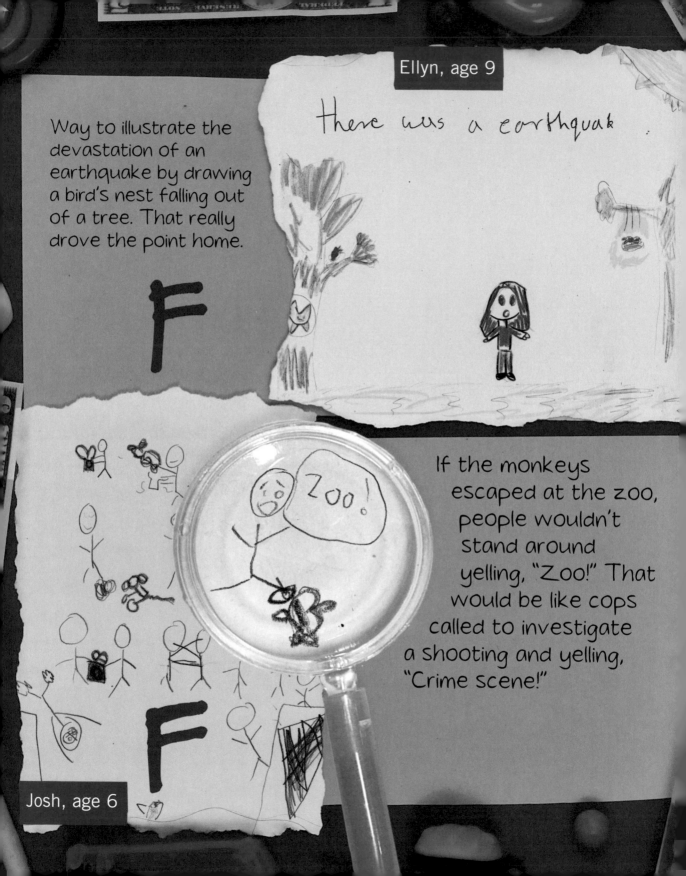

Homeless
people

I agree with this statement.

F+

The Most Beautiful Person or Thing in the World

Stop the press! Turns out kids are narcissists. When they were asked to draw their idea of who the most beautiful boy or girl in the world was, most of the kids drew themselves. I like to think these are pretty spot-on:

Gay.

F

Lee, age 8

Slut.

F

Suzi, age 8

255

Name _____

This Is How I Look

Summer, age 6

I know dick about fashion, but I feel like if I were a six-year-old girl, I'd know not to wear things like trapezoid aprons and square turtlenecks. Maybe just wear some shoes to cover up those stumpy monkey toes. Something.

F

256

Matthew plays Monopoly with his grandma.

Duly noted.

Matthew, age 7

"I'm sorry, your entry into the most beautiful girl in the world contest did not win."

Jamie, age 4

257

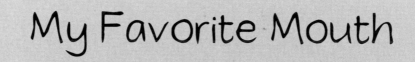

My Favorite Mouth

One of my assignments in high school English class was to write a daily journal entry. I found this especially difficult for a reason that I wouldn't learn until years later after getting the results of a DNA test: I'm genetically averse to busywork. So I would test my teachers to see if they actually read anything I wrote by writing backward, using made-up words with randomly chosen consonants and vowels, copying down receipts, and arranging my sentences in odd geometric shapes. Every entry received the same grade of a "checkmark" for completion. None of it mattered, and the following submissions seem to be no exception.

(F)

Joural: What is your favorite mouth of the year way?

My favorite mouth is February. It's my favorite one because my birthday is in that mouth. Sometimes it rains on my b-day. I could have a party inside with my family. February is a awoesome mouth.

Lots of poeple are born on this mouth. It's also a sweet mouth becaus it's Valentines day. Who wouldn't like February it's so cool. I love this mouth so much. Thats why I pick February as my favorite mouth.

I wouldn't choose to deliver a baby in a mouth, but I suppose it'd do in a pinch. There have been worse things dumped into mouths.

F+

My favorite part of the book is the ending because you find out what happens. That's what I love about the book. It is like a hamburger, but the ending is the juicy part. It is great to read. I don't want to give the ending away.

you
didn't

You have said nothing. You wrote an entire paragraph and literally said nothing. That's actually really hard to do. Hats off.

My favorite restaurant
is Home town buffet. Home
town buffet has ong kind
of food it is so good. They
have like pizza and Hambourgers.
It is also so fancy inside the
restaurant. They also give
very good ice cream.

   In the Icecream
you could put whatever
topings you want. You should
go it is very fancy. Also it has
good meals and desserts for
after you eat. It is my
favorite restaurant in my
Life. That is why you should
go to Home town buffet.

When you're nine years old, saying a place is
the best restaurant you've ever been to in
your life doesn't mean anything. Most babies
would probably rank their mom's titties pretty
high.

F

261

President

If I got voted for president the boys would serve the girls dinner and #1 I would change everything. The boys would do our chores such as, Dishes, grocerie store, dinner, laundry, and our homework I told you I would Change everything!

Sophie-Jasmin, age 11

Bye

Do you honestly think you can win on a platform of making the boys serve the girls dinner? Also, you can't just say "I will change everything" and then say "I told you I would" a few sentences later unless you've actually changed something. Bye!

F

Books by Kids, for Shredders

911 ABOUT me.

1

By Diego

I can run one

2

This book is a two-page autobiography titled "All About Me." It's a description of Diego's ability to walk. Honestly, this is less crappy than most books I've read.

I can Walk

3

The 3nd

4

F+

Diego, age 5

264

The Mouse and Me

Jimmy, age 6

I see a mouse.

The mouse sees me.

We live in a house,

As happy as can be.

If you wrote a story like this in prison, you'd get shanked.

Brev, age 6

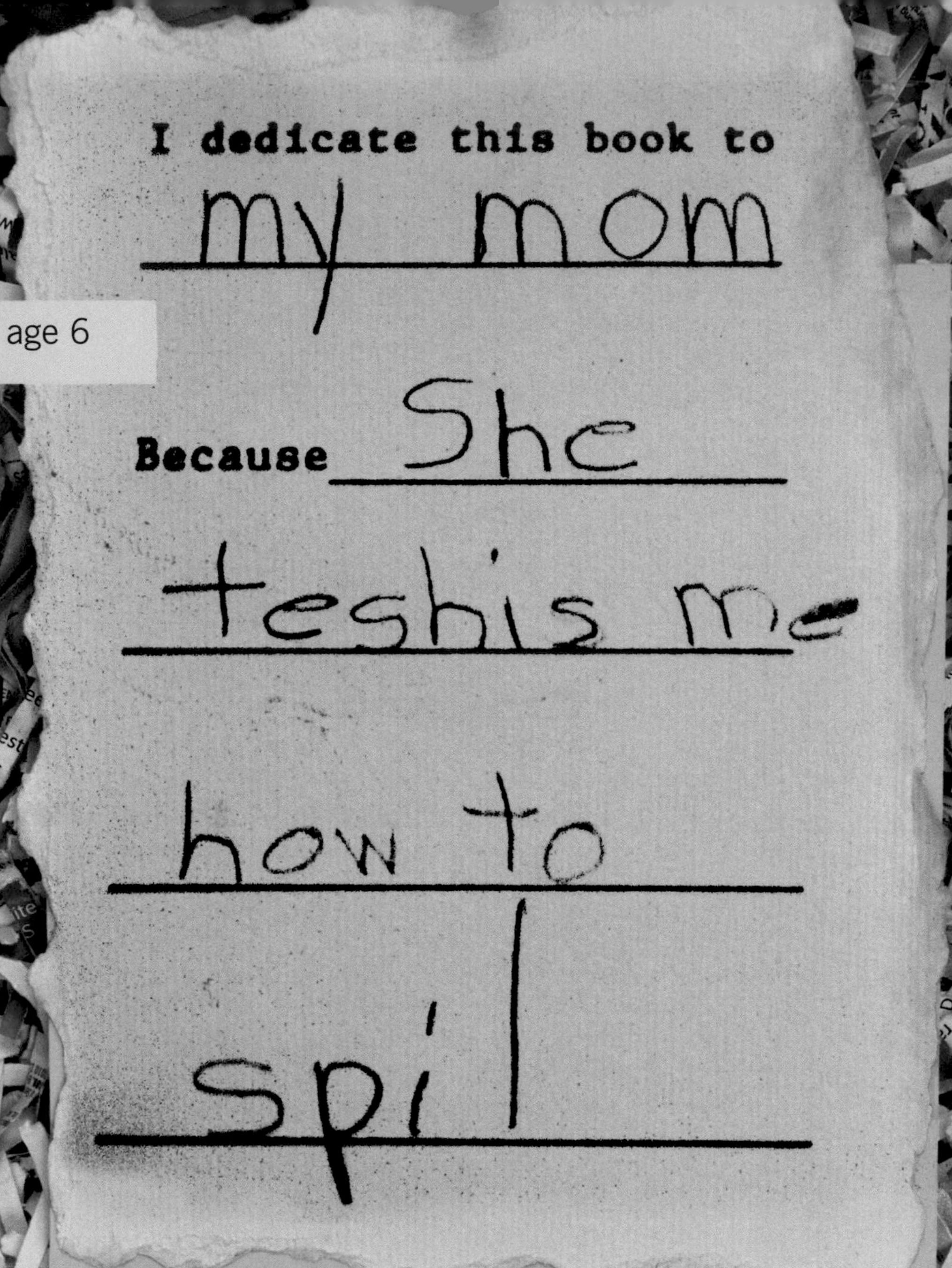

I dedicate this book to my mom

Because She teshis me how to spil

Might want to hold off on that dedication, son.

F

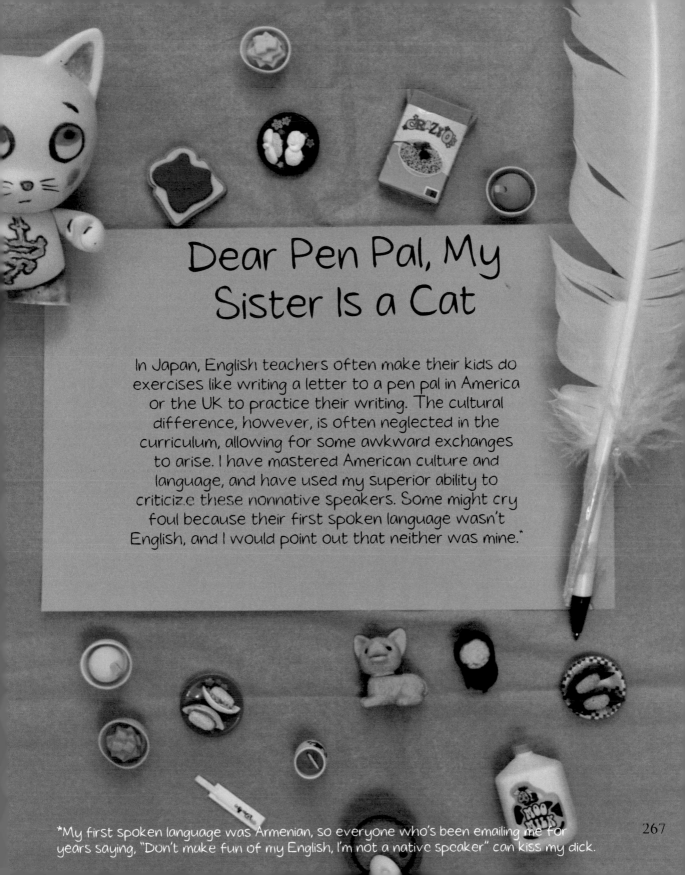

Dear Pen Pal, My Sister Is a Cat

In Japan, English teachers often make their kids do exercises like writing a letter to a pen pal in America or the UK to practice their writing. The cultural difference, however, is often neglected in the curriculum, allowing for some awkward exchanges to arise. I have mastered American culture and language, and have used my superior ability to criticize these nonnative speakers. Some might cry foul because their first spoken language wasn't English, and I would point out that neither was mine.*

*My first spoken language was Armenian, so everyone who's been emailing me for years saying, "Don't make fun of my English, I'm not a native speaker" can kiss my dick.

Dear pen pal
Nice to meet you. I am
Yuichiro. I live in Japan.
In first grade I went
to u.k. so I am good at English.

F

at sports do
u like? I like. soccer.
Do you like fish? I like
fish. My favorite food
is fish. write me back.
YUichiro!!

For a first introduction, topics of discussion usually include what you do, hobbies, and movies you like. But not really fish. In fact, never fish.

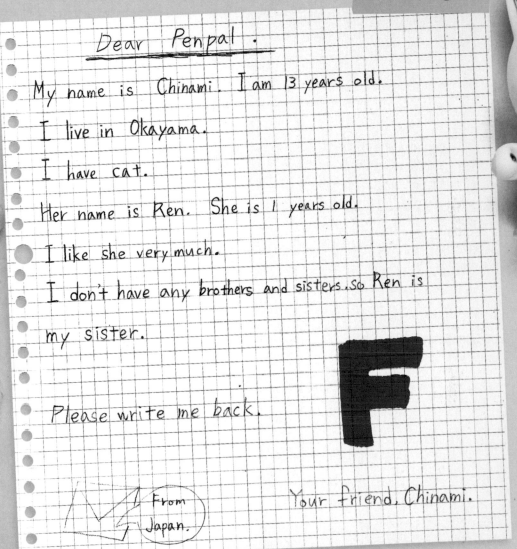

Dear Penpal.

My name is Chinami. I am 13 years old.

I live in Okayama.

I have cat.

Her name is Ren. She is 1 years old.

I like she very much.

I don't have any brothers and sisters. So Ren is

my sister.

F

Please write me back.

From Japan.

Your friend, Chinami.

Dear Chinami, I don't have a sister. I have a brother. So he is my sister. I like she very much. *Arigato!*

269

Yoshiko, age 12

Almost every square inch of this postcard is jam packed with a Japanese cliché. The only thing it's missing is anime speed lines:

Is it racist that I really want ramen right now?

Sexism, Drugs, AIDS and Crib Death

The following are from eighth-grade worksheets on sexism, drugs, AIDS and babies. These are all subjects I excel at.

SEXISM...WHERE DO I FIND IT?

1. Describe what you think sexism is.

Sexism is like racism. ~~racis~~ Sexism is when you are predjuice against someone because of their race. (if you think guys are better than girls at everything, etc)

No, sexism is when you are prejudiced against someone because of their sex. You'd know the answer to this if you were a man.

F

4. Describe one TV commercial or magazine that assumes that women do housework while men have jobs outside the home. How do these assumptions show sexism to both men and women?

~~a~~ a commercial showed women cooking and telling the kids dinners ready. then the dad comes home from "hard day at work." this sexism because women can have mens jobs and vice-versa

Both the question and the answer are wrong. Just because you see a housemom on TV doesn't mean they think all women are housemoms. Assumptions are different from depictions, you idiots.

F-

8. List some symptoms of withdrawal from drugs?

fussy
diarrean
not sleeping good
learning problems
irritable
crib death

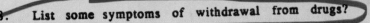

Rolene, age 14

No. Crib death is not a symptom of drug withdrawal, unless you mean the mother's Prozac?

F

Athena, age 13

SEXISM AND SEX-ROLE STEREOTYPING

Quickly read through each statement and mark the response that best fits your opinion. Your choices are: Strongly Agree, Agree, Disagree, and Strongly Disagree.

	Strongly Agree	Agree	Disagree	Strongly Disagree
3. Boys' athletics are really more important than girls'.	👍👍	👍	👎	(👎👎)
4. Men sometimes treat women like playthings.	(👍👍)	👍	👎	👎👎
14. Women make good construction workers and engineers.	(👍👍)	👍	👎	👎👎

This is objectively true. The NFL has about $9 billion in annual revenue, and would rank somewhere around number 260 on the Fortune 500. No women's sport comes close.

What would it even mean to strongly disagree with this?

It's not even controversial to say that women are physically weaker than men and generally don't make good construction workers for that reason. Facts aren't inherently sexist.

F

273

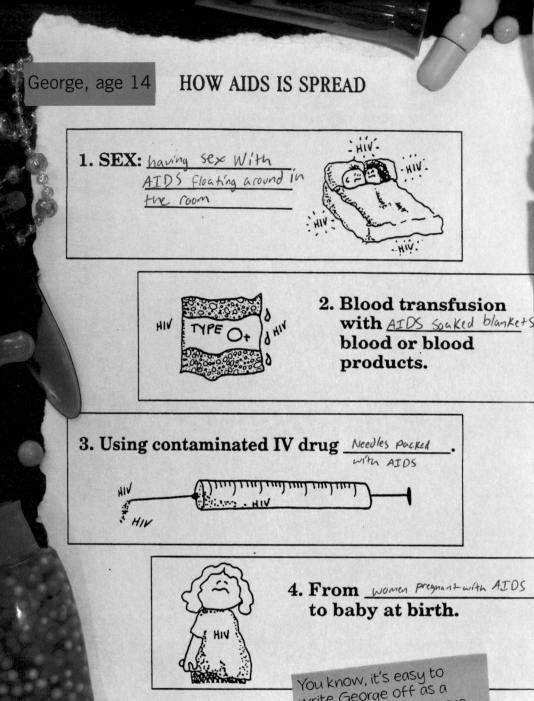

George, age 14

HOW AIDS IS SPREAD

1. **SEX:** having sex with AIDS floating around in the room

2. **Blood transfusion with** AIDS soaked blankets **blood or blood products.**

TYPE O+

3. **Using contaminated IV drug** Needles packed with AIDS.

4. **From** women pregnant with AIDS **to baby at birth.**

You know, it's easy to write George off as a smart-ass, but these are all literal interpretations of the illustrations and I blame the test maker for lack of clarity, not the test taker.

F+ for George, and
F- for the worksheet.

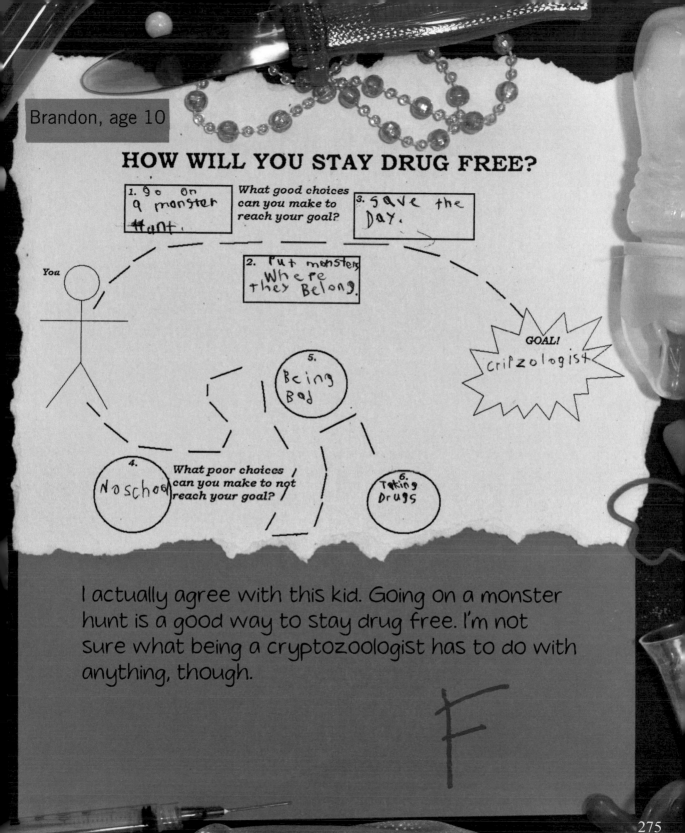

Brandon, age 10

HOW WILL YOU STAY DRUG FREE?

1. go on a monster Hunt.

What good choices can you make to reach your goal?

3. Save the Day.

You

2. Put monsters Where they Belong.

5. Being Bad

GOAL!
cripzologist

4. No school

What poor choices can you make to not reach your goal?

6. Taking Drugs

I actually agree with this kid. Going on a monster hunt is a good way to stay drug free. I'm not sure what being a cryptozoologist has to do with anything, though.

F

11. A good anti-PCP slogan/message is <u>Some call it Angel Dust, some call it Love Boat, we call it PcP-suicide.</u>

F

Ren, age 13

This slogan is lazy because you could put almost any word next to "suicide" to make it seem negative; for example, kitten suicide and Disney suicide. The one exception may be lesbian orgy suicide, which is always positive.

14. How can teens say no to PCP?

<u>Just to not go anywhere where there might be PcP</u>

Why not suggest that people avoid dying by not going to places where they'll die?

F

Brian says notodrugs

Brian, age 10

but yes to Bananas

More like "yes to boners."

F

Celebrities

Shane, age 16

The resemblance to Will Smith is uncanny; I knew this was him right away.

F+

This is supposed to be Will Smith's mom. I've never met the lady, so this might be spot-on.

F+

Shane, age 16

Yes we can

Gardner, age 11

Our commander in chief: a giant, robotic golfing puppet. Or is he peeing? In any case, F

Albert, age 12

Obama might look like this if a cartoon cigar exploded in his face. Racist.

F-

Brian, age 5

I'm 60% sure SpongeBob didn't have herpes on the TV show.

F

There are no angels where he's going.

F

nikal Jackson

Gabbie, age 8

Jerkbook

Ever wonder why you keep in touch with only four or five friends from high school? If so, go back and read your yearbook comments to be reminded: everyone was a huge gristly dick to you all the time. Here are a few examples:

Have a good summer. — Just Kidding.
Josh

Hey, Josh, hope you don't get abducted from your family while traveling in Europe over the summer. Just kidding.

F

Sorry we didn't ~~get to~~ know each other befor, but at least we laughed at each other. I hope you don't get kicked out of college
deni

F

If "bitchiness" were a category, this entry would win the Pulitzer Prize.

I'm the first one to write on this page how cool is that? Well I'll see ya next year!

Love ya,

Pedro ☺

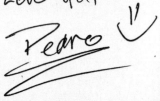

Pedro, age 14

This is the yearbook equivalent of douchebags who comment "first" on forums.

F

Jordan, age 18

What up Baby? How you doing? It was tight getting to know you in photography. Keep working out hooters so you can hook me up with some wings! Good luck after high school. Call me up if you need a quickie! PEACE JORDAN

You're not only offering to let her risk her job, but then she gets to have sex with you? Give this man a cigar.

F+

"Hello, Natasha? Hi, this is Person from middle school? Shut up! I was just thinking about you too!"

F

dear person, thanx for being such a great freind. My phone #'s on page 53 Live long!!

Natasha

Natasha, age 15

Marie,
Thanks for being
a good friend. It
was fun, I hope you
in my first period.

Marie
Have a good
summer see
next year
                Albert
"ODD"

Hey Marie!
you are
person, and
sorry to see y
leave. Good luck
year and to the
to come! love, amand

HEY MARIE!
I DIDN'T REALLY
GET TO TALK TO YOU
BUT THAT'S OKAY. HAVE
A FUN SUMMER... KAY!

RYAN

Marie -
It was really great
having you in my 2nd.
e to see you
ext year if you go.

see ya,
Daniel

Marie,
I'll miss
everyone else
will be going
CHEESECAKE, I
you have fun

Dear Marie,
was up... when high
school are you going
too? Hope you have
a high ass summer

Hey, Ryan, if someone didn't
really talk to you, how about
not taking up 50% of the
yearbook page saying so?
Actually, this seems like
something I would do. I take
that back.

Ryan, age 13

F+

285

Unintentional
Bukkake

Cindi, age 9

It may be hard to tell from this photo, but this beaver is textured with jizzy white lumps:

It looks like the entire drawing was made using a palette of brown, blue, and bukkake. Although the effect was probably unintentional, the fact that it's a beaver doesn't help.

You don't get to be king of the jungle covered in buckets of ejaculate.

Cindi, age 9

F

288

Child Prodigies or
COCKSURE IDIOTS?

Kimberly, age 12

This would be great if humans had two eyes of different shapes and sizes on their heads. But they don't, so it's not. Too bad you drew this in marker. Oh well, start over.

F

Tiana, age 9

Way to sneak the one thing you know how to draw into a holiday it has nothing to do with.

F

Remie, age 12

Look at that neck! Was Jesus a wrestler? Also, why does Jesus look vaguely intrigued?

F

Maria, age 10

Finding fish in a pond this small is unlikely in a deciduous, broadleaf forest. Did you mean to draw a temperate rain forest, you fucking idiot?

F-

Art, age 11

I don't think there has ever been a book about a bear confessing his dementia to a psychiatrist, but this would be an awesome start to that book.

F+

Kelly, age 15

Maybe she was born with it. Maybe it's Maybelline.

F

293

Ashley, age 8

By smearing shit on your art, you've basically done my job for me.

F+

Kyly, age 4

"What do you mean I can't use the hall pass until I finish my art project? Okay, done! But I don't need the hall pass anymore."

F

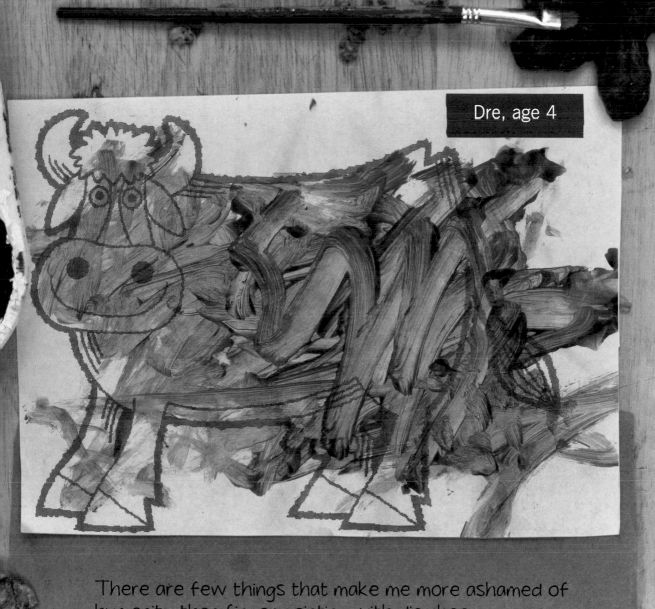

There are few things that make me more ashamed of humanity than finger painting with diarrhea.

Draw Your Favorite Food

orange

strawberry

cherry

F

Grace, age 7

Oh really? Is a strawberry the size of a pineapple? No, microbitch, it isn't. Am I the last person on earth who still gives a shit about what words mean?

Clit-flavored ice cream sounds like a hot mess, and this is coming from a guy whose food pyramid has pussy at the top.

F

Will, age 6

We All Scream For Ice Cream!

I like ice cream Because it is good
My favorite is co klit

299

William, age 5

F A hammer is not a food.

I don't know what's less appetizing: the steaming plates of turds, or Monica's projectile drool.

F

Monica

yum!

Monica, age 12

Young Maddox

Between teachers who confiscated and threw away most of my artwork, and my uncooperative parents who won't give up any (they're not my biggest fans), I've only been able to salvage a few pieces from my childhood. Still, they kick balls full-time.

Maddox, age 11

Fuck yeah, now that's a badass car! This car makes bitches moan, and if they don't, blows them the fuck away with the .50-caliber machine-gun horns. I didn't draw the dinosaur, or the wheels, or the machine guns, but I pasted the shit out of all three using Microsoft Paint. I did draw the gunfire though, which is rather choice.

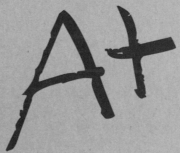

What a great invention.

A+

Maddox, age 13

Just a wrestler dropping a wicked elbow bomb on a bull's back. No big deal.

A+

Maddox, age 11

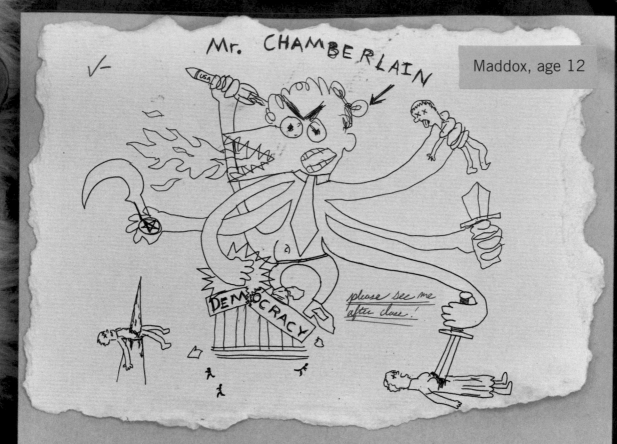

Mr. CHAMBERLAIN

Maddox, age 12

please see me after class!

DEMOCRACY

This is a portrait of my sixth-grade teacher, Mr. Chamberlain. He had a black belt in being an asshole. He confiscated a notebook full of my sketches one time because I was drawing a badass dragon, and he thought it was related to the pencil-and-paper role-playing game, Dungeons & Dragons, supposed to be affiliated with satanic worship by dumbass parents and church groups. When I asked for my notebook back after school, he said he'd thrown it away.

A+ for me   F- for Mr. Chamberlain

Cooking with Minors

Matt and Ian,
ages 14 and 15

Corn, huge chunks of runny tomato, and ham is 50% of what my vomit is comprised of. The other 50% is Tabasco sauce and rum. And yet my vomit never looks this bad.

F

F

Miranda, age 5

This gave my mouth the opposite of a boner.

Maddox, age 32

That's right, bitch! IT'S MOTHERFUCKING LATTICE-TOP APPLE PIE FROM SCRATCH. I read countless forums and recipes written by women complaining about how hard it is to make the crust:

"Waaah, the lattice is hard to make, waaah, my arthritis!" Ninety percent of the lattice-top pies you see have strips of crust lazily thrown on top of each other. That's because your grandma sucks at baking. That's right, I'm not just better than your kids, I am better than your grandma! I can't believe how much I rule.

A+

Acknowledgments

First and foremost, I would like to thank Marie Valenzuela. On a scale of 1 to 10, with 10 being the highest level of importance in getting this book done, and 0 being the least, she'd get a billion. She helped with almost every aspect of this book. If it's in the book, she probably had something to do with it. From color correction and scanning to busting my balls to get it done, she made everything possible. I can't overstate her importance, or succinctly give her the gratitude she's due in the pages allotted to me in this book.

Next is Marie Barr, the genius behind all of the layouts for this project. Every toy, marble, or scrap of paper that you see in this book was carefully selected, arranged and photographed by her. Her studio looked like it was carpet bombed with children by the time she finished this book. Working with her is like hitting the talent lottery. Check her out at: http://mariebarr.com/

Thanks to Nort Mahoney for tirelessly scanning hundreds of drawings, giving unlimited support and encouragement (the real kind, not the phony shit parents give to kids), and giving the most thorough notes and edits on my manuscript of anyone, next to my actual editor. Nort is a badass and as selfless and giving as people get. Especially when it comes to his unearthly flatulence, which he has in abundance.

Special thanks to Assistant Designer, and longtime friend, Roger Barr, who helped tirelessly edit the artwork into the layouts for this book. Roger has been creating some of the best video games and writeups of shitty b-movies for over a decade. Check out his awesome site at: http://www.i-mockery.com

A big thanks to my friend Kevin Creech, who did an incredible job blending artwork into the layouts. Kevin edited a huge chunk of this book and is the fastest and most accurate person I've ever seen use Photoshop. The man is a machine. Thanks also to Jack Allison, Don Smith, and Dax Herrera also for doing a kickass job editing artwork into the layouts. I had less than three weeks to edit all the artwork, and couldn't have done it without them.

Thanks to all my close friends who helped me pull this through, with contributions from the aforementioned as well as Brian Cooperman, and Cheryl Liebert. They sat up late with me to work on the book on more than one occasion, and I couldn't have asked for a better crew to work with. Their creativity and endless generosity with their time almost softens my emotionally hardened heart. Thanks to Brian, Nort, Deborah Tarica and Dax Herrera for helping proofread. They tolerated unwieldy 400-page binders to give me notes.

And speaking of talent, thanks to Robyn Von Swank for her excellent author photo and cover suggestions. Thanks to Darryl Pierce, Matt Parker, Misty Bruce, and Angelo Vildasol for their help in promotion and Facebook administration. Thanks to my great friend and fellow pirate, Leah Tiscione, for her help in reaching out to badasses.

I was lucky enough to work with my friend and editor from "The Alphabet of Manliness," Jeremie Ruby-Strauss. He pulled double duty this time as my agent and editor when he wasn't busy slaying fools with his wit. The guy still just gets it. He has the rare ability to persuade people, and the even rarer ability to be persuaded. Talent of his caliber is rare in not just publishing, but any industry.

Thanks to Ashly Kersch, Alex and Diego Aguirre, Jonathan and Amanda Joyce, Nicki Diamond, Alice Huguet, Jess Valenzuela, Harrison Brown, Gwen Uszuko and Jason Hedrich for their contributions, friendship, and support.

And a BIG FUCKING THANK YOU TO ME for paging this entire book by myself. Yes, in a publishing first for me (and possibly the publisher), I did triple duty by editing the layouts and formatting the entire book for print—in addition to writing it. If I don't give myself credit here, nobody else will. Hats off to you, Maddox. You really pulled through on this one. And you are good looking.

And thanks to Danny Kilpatrick and everyone else who submitted to me online. Your artwork was terrible. Without your children's lack of talent, this book wouldn't be possible. Thank you, and get better.

And finally, no thanks to Austin Blank who helped with absolutely nothing.